Getting Apart Together

Getting Apart Together

The Couple's Guide
to a Fair Divorce or Separation

Martin A. Kranitz, M.A.

Impact Publishers,® Inc.

ATTENTION ORGANIZATIONS AND CORPORATIONS:
This book is available at quantity discounts on bulk purchases for educational, business, or sales promotional use. For further information, please contact Impact Publishers, P.O. Box 6016, Atascadero, CA 93423-6016, Phone: 1-800-246-7228, e-mail: sales@impactpublishers.com

Library of Congress Cataloging-in-Publication Data

Kranitz, Martin A. (Martin Alan), 1942-
  Getting apart together : the couple's guide to a fair divorce or separation / Martin A. Kranitz.
      p. cm.
  Includes bibliographical references and index.
  ISBN 1-886230-21-8 (alk. paper)
    1. Divorce--United States. 2. Divorce settlements--United States--Hand-books, manuals, etc. 3. Divorce mediation--United States--Handbooks, manuals, etc. I. Title.

HQ834 .K73 2000
306.89--dc21   00-022260

Publisher's Note
This publication is designed to provide accurate and authoritative information in regard to the subject matter covered. It is sold with the understanding that the publisher is not engaged in rendering psychological, legal, financial, or other professional services. If expert assistance or counseling is needed, the services of a competent professional should be sought.

Impact Publishers and colophon are registered trademarks of Impact Publishers, Inc.

Cover design by Sharon Schnare, San Luis Obispo, California.
Printed in the United States of America on acid-free paper,

Published by *Impact*  *Publishers*®

An Imprint of
newharbingerpublications, inc.
5674 Shattuck Avenue • Oakland CA 94609 • USA
800-748-6273 • fax 510-652-5472
www.newharbinger.com

Contents

PREFACE

THE GOAL OF THIS BOOK is to provide you with practical information you can use in resolving the issues that arise when people who have lived together decide to separate. These issues are basically the same whether you were married or living together. If there are children, parenting is a concern, as are property, child and spousal support, health and life insurance, education, and taxes.

Each of the topics covered in the chapters include both a discussion of the issues and a presentation of options and alternatives for dealing with the topic. The options are presented in the form of scenarios, with background information, so that you can see what the parties are attempting to accomplish.

It is my hope that by using this book, you will be able to deal with the issues of separation and divorce in a collaborative, rather than competitive, fashion. The process will be less painful, but not pain-free. Working together to figure things out is not easy, but it is doable and definitely worthwhile. If you've received this book from your mediator, you'll want to read through the entire book quickly to get a sense of what is covered, and then read each appropriate chapter prior to the session in which you will discuss those topics. For this book to work, it is best that you read the chapter well in advance (not the night before your session). That way you will have a chance to carefully consider what you have read, and perhaps come up with other ideas for discussion.

What I Have Learned

I was quite pleased when Dr. Bob Alberti contacted me indicating an interest in updating and re-releasing this book. In the twelve years since the first edition of this book was published, I've learned a lot from my clients. This edition incorporates what I have learned, including a number of additional issues that have been raised by couples going through separation and divorce.

I've been a family mediator for nearly two decades, and it is clearer now than ever before how much emotional pain accompanies separation and divorce. It interferes with our ability to think, communicate, and function — even at the most basic level — at a time when it is most crucial for us to problem-solve and deal with issues of family survival. *Feeling rejected hurts.* So does feeling betrayed, alone, or ill-equipped to support yourself. It is not fun. It may surprise you to learn that it is just as painful and just as scary for the person who suggests separation as for the person who has separation forced upon him or her. In spite of this, it is possible for people who want to maintain some control in their lives to get through this difficult time.

About Revenge. Separation and divorce, which are almost unavoidably painful, may lead those in pain to strike out at those around them. When you are hurting, you might say things to hurt others. *Control Yourself!* The momentary pleasure one reaps in seeing a partner's discomfort will quickly turn sour. In all likelihood you will eventually ask, "Why was I such a jerk?" "How could I say such a stupid thing?" Negative comments will rapidly escalate the hostility. It's not worth long-term aggravation to experience short-term satisfaction. If hostilities escalate to a very high level, the relationship necessary to continue parenting may be irretrievably damaged. When this happens, every interaction between the parents becomes a competition, rather than collaboration, for child rearing. This results in a waste of energy which could be better focused on your child(ren). The more you fuss with each other, the less time you have for your child(ren) and yourselves. You have plenty to do just getting on with your own life.

About Sounding Off. In many relationships partners learn to avoid unnecessary conflict by "tip-toeing" around the other party's objectionable behavior. We bite our tongues and avoid saying the things we are thinking in order to avoid unnecessary hostilities. Often, after separation, there is a tendency for people to think, "I don't have to put up with his crap anymore!" "I don't have to put up with her being late, disrespectful, critical, or irresponsible." Not true. For better or for worse, you *will* still need to deal with the "crap." If there are children involved, you will need to deal with each other (and each other's crap) for a long period of time. *Get used to it!* The world is not perfect, your partner is not perfect, and neither are you. Even if there are no children, keep a lid on it until after the negotiations are finished. Why rock the boat? Why say something that will decrease the likelihood of getting what you — and your child(ren) need? Wait until the negotiations are done and the documents are signed, then, while the ink is drying, express your opinions — if you still feel you must. If you are like most people — and have waited that long — you will probably no longer feel the need to say it at all. What is more important... the urge to cause pain or the need to survive? There is another important consideration here that should not be overlooked. The greater the friction between the parents, the greater the likelihood that the child(ren) will also be brought into the conflict, either as participants or pawns. In either event, they are the ones that are most likely to suffer the most trauma. Children don't know that life is not fair and that, on occasion, your conflict with your ex will bite you in the butt. *The higher the level of conflict, the more likely it is that the child(ren) will suffer psychological damage.* It's okay for you to be upset with another person; it's not okay to put your children in the middle of the war zone just for the sake of getting back at the other parent.

About Dealing with Your Emotions. Keep in mind that, for most people, it is not easy or pleasant to consider separation or divorce. This goes for the initiator as well as the non-initiator. There are a number of emotional stages that people go through when dealing with separation and divorce.

If you find that you are having trouble getting control of your feelings of anger, resentment, fear, rejection or any other negative emotion, you may want to read *Rebuilding: When Your Relationship Ends* (Fisher & Alberti), *50 Ways to Love Your Leaver* (Webb), or *How to Make Yourself Happy and Remarkably Less Disturbable* (Ellis). If your emotions are really out of control, think about talking to a counselor or therapist to help you deal with your feelings. Check with friends, relatives or neighbors to see which counselors they recommend. Check with your local "Y," church, synagogue, or service organization for the names of support groups in your area.

About the Children. When children are involved there are other issues that need to be considered:
- Children have a right to a relationship with both parents
- Children need to feel loved by each parent, and a part of both parents' household
- Perhaps the other parent doesn't love you anymore, but that doesn't mean she doesn't love the children
- The fact that the other parent wasn't involved in the children's activities in the past doesn't mean he shouldn't be involved now
- Children don't want to hear negative things about their parents... even from you!
- Studies show that parents who criticize each other in front of the children (or who are overheard criticizing the other parent) are likely to be seen as manipulative and controlling, and may be rejected by the children. Bad-mouthing the other parent is more likely to come back and haunt you, rather than do harm to the other parent. Don't risk losing the respect and trust of your children.
- We all live multidimensional lives. A parent's behavior in areas that have nothing to do with parenting ability should not be held against the parent when dealing with parenting issues.

It is possible to work together as a mother and father, even though you cannot live together as husband and wife.

About Courts and Lawyers. Litigation, by its very nature, is a conflict of interest. The longer a lawyer can keep the conflict going, the more the lawyer gets paid. It is not uncommon for lawyers to drag things out (in the name of getting the best deal), and then suggest or force a settlement on the courthouse steps because:
- they realize the case is not that strong.
- most of the family assets have been used up in litigation and they won't get paid for any more time.
- they acknowledge that courts can be fickle, and fair outcomes are unpredictable.

Most judges and lawyers will tell you that there are no winners in divorce court. They recognize that *the best family decisions are made by the couple involved.* (For confirmation of this, I recommend Judge James Stewart's *Child Custody Book*, especially chapters 3 and 13 on relationships with lawyers in custody matters.) If a lawyer tells you she can "get you this" or "promise you that" in court, ask her to guarantee it, and put in writing that she won't charge you for going to court if you don't get what she promises. Chances are pretty good that she will refuse.

If you do go to court, you'll not only spend a lot of money you can ill afford, you will encounter a number of additional transaction costs as well, including:

• *Time* — away from your work and family — spent both in court and with your lawyer in preparation for court.

• The *distraction* that will occur when your mind is on the litigation.

• *Lost opportunities* to do other things (either fun- or work-related) because your time and money have been spent on the litigation process.

• *Increased hostility* for and difficulty dealing with your partner after the judge has made a decision.

Keep in mind that even if the court were to make the most perfect decision in the world concerning your family, once you have vocalized those terrible comments (which you may be encouraged to say in court to win your case), it will be immensely difficult to continue working with each other to raise your children. Your chances of getting the outcome that you think is best for the family are greater when you have input and take control of the decision-making process. This occurs when the two of you talk together, either between yourselves or in mediation. Once you go to court you are no longer in control. Ask yourself this question, *"Do I want someone who does not know my family or love my children to make decisions about what will happen in my family?"* Most people do not. That is why they try to avoid court by working things out between themselves or with the aid of the mediator. They discover that it's usually best to bite their tongues or leave the room rather than respond to inappropriate, untrue, or critical comments.

If You Need Help
This book is designed to help you reduce conflict and improve your working relationship with "the other party." The chapters review the most common practical issues partners need to address in a separation or divorce. Every family situation is unique, of

course, so you may have issues specific to you that you won't find addressed here. Approach them in the same way you would any of the other issues in this book.

• Talk about the issue with your ex until you are clear what both of you must consider.

• Brainstorm options and alternatives until you feel you have a fair representation of possibilities.

• Select an option that is acceptable to both of you.

• Record your decisions so that you can make reference to them when necessary.

I encourage you to seek the services of a competent professional mediator, should your discussions become overwhelming. And I wish you good luck.

Sincerely,
Martin Kranitz
Annapolis, Maryland, Autumn 2000

Acknowledgements

To MY FAMILY (Yvonne, Elyse, Genna and Maddison) for their support. To my clients and students who have taught me more than they will ever know. My thanks to Bob Alberti and Impact Publishers for allowing me the opportunity to update this book and to make it available (once again) to families in need, and to Thad Toal, CPA, of Toal, Ranes, Davis and Simmons for again reviewing the tax chapter. Finally, my thanks goes to friends and associates in the field of family mediation who have worked with me to forward acceptance of family mediation both in courts and private practice for the last twenty years.

— Martin Kranitz

Introduction for Mediators

THIS BOOK WAS ORIGINALLY WRITTEN FOR COUPLES to use in working through the issues of separation and divorce. My experience as a mediator had convinced me that *many* couples could work things out between themselves if they knew what to talk about (the issues), and what alternatives (the options) existed.

Since that time I have found another use for the book. As you know, *not all* couples can work things out by themselves, but still want to avoid the litigation maze. These people often seek out or are referred to a family mediator. I'm confident you'll find this book as useful to your mediation clients as it is to partners working on their own.

Many mediators already use *Getting Apart Together* as a workbook to guide client homework assignments during the mediation process. Some provide the book to their clients at the first session as part of their "orientation package," others purchase copies to resell to their clients, and still others "lease" the book to their clients, asking for a deposit to be returned when mediation is over and the book is returned.

Both the mediator and the clients benefit from review of the material, which helps them to understand the issues and some of the options discussed during mediation sessions. Of course, the options presented in this book are not the only options available, but merely a sampling of some creative solutions.

If you decide to use this book in mediation or recommend it to your clients, there are several ways that you can proceed. You can give an outline of instructions at the first session, asking the parties to read the appropriate chapter for topics to be discussed at a particular session, or remind the parties to read a chapter appropriate for the next session at the end of each session.

The chapters in this book are arranged in the same order that most family mediators use to cover pertinent issues: parenting, property, support, insurance, education, and taxes.

If you are interested in purchasing *Getting Apart Together*, for your clients, it is available at quantity discount through the publisher. Contact Impact Publishers, Inc., at 1-800-246-7228 or info@impactpublishers.com

I hope you'll find this book useful for your mediation clients and I welcome any feedback. I look forward to hearing from you.

— Martin Kranitz

1

Ground Rules
First, You Lay the Foundation

BEFORE WE START TALKING ABOUT SPECIFICS, there are some general ground rules that you and your spouse (partner) should know and agree to in order to facilitate your working together. This will take some effort and may not be easy, but it is something you can both accomplish together. The fact that you may not have agreed on everything — or anything — in the past, doesn't mean that you won't be successful here. You will increase your chances for success by making a commitment to try.

• *You'll need to set up specific times for discussion of the issues of separation and divorce,* whether you are still living together or are already separated. Ideally, once or twice a week is about the maximum, unless discussions are going exceptionally well.

It is important that you make every attempt to meet at the appointed time and be prepared with whatever homework has been discussed and agreed upon. Take care not to be unrealistic in terms of setting homework assignments. Keep in mind that this is a very stressful and difficult time for both of you. When you're under stress, things often take longer to accomplish than they normally would. This does not, however, give either of you license to drag your feet or put off gathering information in order to avoid dealing with the realities of the separation. Within reason, the more quickly you can get things accomplished, as long as they are done properly and accurately, the more smoothly the process will go.

• *Set and follow an agenda so you'll know exactly what you are going to discuss at each meeting.* There are sample agendas in Appendix A which may be copied on to larger sheets of paper for use during discussion, or you may wish to make a photocopy from the book and use the back of the page for notes.

• *You will probably find it helpful to discuss the topics in the order presented in this book.* Experience has shown this order useful, especially if you can compartmentalize (that is, talk about each issue separately, without tying it into the other issues or sub-issues). Everything is connected, ultimately, but you can't talk about everything at once. Discuss the issues one at a time, in order, separately. After you have a sense of how both of you are going to handle an issue, you can start to fine-tune it later, as it relates to other decisions you have made.

• *Co-parenting* is the first topic because it is best to take the children out of the war zone. Try to look at parenting issues as a function of the children's needs, rather than tying them directly to financial matters. Sure, there is a connection, but you are going to continue to be parents, regardless of how much money the family has. Besides, there are resources other than money that can be used to help support the family. Deal with "policy issues" first — co-parenting and the various contact schedules — then later, at the appropriate time, deal with how those policies can be best accomplished from a financial standpoint. Recognize that "to get the house," "to get more support," or "to pay less support" are very poor reasons for wanting to keep the children with you. Keep the issues separate, as much as possible, and you will find that things progress more smoothly and that you will end up with a more reasonable and more equitable arrangement — for the children and for yourselves.

• *Topic areas should be broken down into the smallest increments possible.* For example, trying to discuss the whole topic of co-parenting at once would be a useless and frustrating experience. Breaking the co-parenting issues into component parts will be much more productive. See Appendix A for list of co-parenting topics.

• *There are no "right" or "wrong" answers.* No two households operate exactly the same, and no two families parent in the same way. Even parents living under the same roof often have different perspectives on how to handle things. It is useful to come in with an open mind, a willingness to discuss common issues, work together, and negotiate until a mutually-agreeable solution is found. Keep in mind, even then, the solution may have to be adjusted at a later date, since your needs — and the needs of your children — may change.

• *"Discussion" means the give-and-take of information with both parties listening and talking.* It does not mean one person telling the other person how things are going to be. Try using "I" statements rather than "you" statements. "You" statements (you always, you never, you didn't, you have to) are typically heard as critical, punitive and diminishing. They are usually about the past, and the past cannot be changed. Because of the negative implications of "you" statements, many people become defensive and either discount the idea or stop listening altogether, thereby missing the point. "I" statements (I'd prefer this, I don't care for that, I would like to look at more options) reflect what you think or you feel, and are perspectives to which you are entitled. The person hearing your view is not as likely to be threatened, and therefore is more likely to hear the content — the pearls of wisdom — and respond less defensively.

• *Focus on the present and the future.* You can't change the past, so why spend all of your time talking about it? Focus on today and tomorrow. Use the past only as a springboard for how to make tomorrow better. If you didn't like the way something was done in the past, talk about how it can be improved, not what you didn't like about it. The more you can frame your comments in positive language about positive outcomes, rather than focusing on unsatisfactory past behavior, the more likely it is that you will both come to an understanding that works for all involved.

• *Check your communication effectiveness periodically.* If you find that you and your spouse are in very strong emotional disagreement, look at what it is that you are "discussing" and determine first whether you have strayed from the topic. If you have, stop talking about whatever it was and return to the topic. If you are on topic, then take a look at whether you both really are talking about the same thing. Couples often believe that they are communicating well, when, in fact, each has an entirely different perception of what they are talking about. *Take the time to define the issue in some detail, and have the other person repeat what he heard so that you can be more assured that you are talking about the same topic.* If he does not re-state what you said accurately (not necessarily word for word), repeat your definition using different words, and ask him to re-state again when you finish. *Don't proceed to the problem-solving piece until you are both clear that you understand the topic at hand.*

• *Both spouses need to agree that either one has permission to discontinue the discussion (negotiation) at any time, for any reason whatsoever.* If a discussion is discontinued because your partner becomes angry or upset, for example, do not try to force or cajole her into continuing the discussion; it may not be emotionally possible. It is a good idea to set up a subsequent appointment for continued discussion. There may be an agreement that the discussion will be started again in an hour, in a day, in three days, in a week, or whatever seems reasonable and convenient for both parties.

A person who chooses to discontinue the discussion ought not be pressed nor feel obligated to explain why she has discontinued the session. Stopping a negotiation session is not to be used as a technique for avoiding separation. As long as the discussion is going reasonably well, keep it going (even if you're not in favor of the separation). Things could get worse. It could become more difficult to communicate and negotiate. As the saying goes, "Make hay while the sun shines."

• *On the other hand, sessions ought to last only one-and-a-half to two hours, even if discussions are going rather well.* Experience has shown that longer periods of discussion usually will not produce useful or positive results. Don't hesitate to stop the discussion even earlier if you have run out of things to talk about. If you have covered the agenda set for a particular session, or find that you don't have enough information to discuss the topic further, move along to the next topic. If you're unable or unprepared to discuss the next topic, end the session.

• *Remember that decisions reached in discussion are only tentative,* and can be changed, renegotiated, or modified right up until the final separation or divorce agreement is signed. You need to have a tentative decision so that you know in what direction to proceed. It is even possible to make agreements on a contingent basis. That is, you could agree that "Plan A" will take effect if "X" and "Y" occur, and "Plan B" will take effect if "Z" occurs. In this way you can cover several bases without having to renegotiate each time a life change takes place.

• *It's important that you both keep a record of what you decide on during the course of your discussions.* Write down your understanding of the tentative decisions on each issue, and read it to your spouse to accept, correct, or modify as needed. Make sure you have enough detail. This is especially important if you're working without the aid of a professional. Your agreement will, in all likelihood, be turned into a legal document. This document will become binding and enforceable. You will need the detail to avoid confusion and misunderstanding in the future.

• *Homework is an important part of the process that consists of both thinking and doing.* At times, it will involve thinking about and writing down ideas (options) for handling particular issues; at other times you will be gathering additional information needed to discuss topics or make informed decisions. Specific homework is difficult to assign, since your progress will depend upon your unique circumstances. At the end of each session, set up an agenda for the following session, note what information will be needed in the next discussion, decide what material each of you will gather, and assign your homework accordingly. Write down these homework assignments to avoid later confusion. It is also a good idea for each of you to write down your ideas or proposals for future discussion as they occur to you between sessions, rather than trying to remember everything and working out of your head. You may want to carry around a little notebook to record your ideas and issues. They tend to pop up at the strangest times. If you both regularly bring to your meetings written alternatives for the issues being discussed, you will be able to see concretely the similarities and differences, and to discuss the pros and cons more rationally.

In general, it is a good idea to *think in multiples*. By that I mean, look at and think about doing things in different ways. Whether we're talking about parenting schedules or property division, if you come up with only one way to do it, it will be much harder to look at other ideas (especially those proposed by your partner). Rather, try to come up with several different approaches that you can live with for any given issue. If you do this, and your partner does this, you will be much more likely to have an open mind and be better able to look at still other possibilities that you may not have thought of.

• *Neutral Language.* Just as there are "I-messages" and "you-messages," so too can you use other language to help or hinder the communication process. Phrases like " my children", "your fault"," my pension" or "the judge will make you" will, in all likelihood raised the level of friction, hostility and defensiveness. Rather, wherever possible, *use more neutral language* that will help facilitate the communication. Try to use phrases like "our children," "my concern is," "the pension" or "if we don't work this out together, someone we don't know will make decisions, about our family for us." Look at the separation/divorce process as *a mutual problem-solving activity*, in which you and your spouse are equal partners in defining the problem and working toward an answer. This is most important. If you are willing to *work together* toward a resolution, you are much more likely to be successful than if you view the discussion as a battle or a contest to be won or lost. If you can focus on what is best for the family unit as a whole (and all the members of the family unit) — rather than "How much can I get out of this?" — you have a much greater likelihood of success. Neutral and cooperative discussions between spouses can turn into a win-win situation for everyone. This is true regardless of whose idea it was to separate.

• *Get professional help when you need it.* The process of discussion needs to be rational. If either of you find that your emotions are continually interfering with the discussion or the decision-making process, then you need to seriously consider seeking professional help in the form of a professional mediator, or perhaps a mental health counselor or psychotherapist to help you deal with the emotional aspects of what you're experiencing. It is not at all unusual for people going through separation to need the help and support of an outside resource. *"The wise person sees no shame in using a staff for support while walking in difficult terrain."* If you see that you are in difficult terrain, you may also need support to help you through your journey.

"Home Work" for the Co-Parenting Discussion

It helps to have both parents complete each assignment in writing prior to the discussion and to bring the written work to the session. When several items are suggested, prepare two or more variations (options) for discussion.

Reading
Read this "Co-Parenting I" chapter before completing the following assignments. Read and follow the Agenda for this topic provided in Appendix A.

Sharing Information
List information you believe needs to be shared. Note additional information you are willing to share. How will you accomplish the sharing process? (See Children's Data Sheet in Appendix F)

Medical Emergencies
How will medical emergencies be handled? Will you each have a signed permission slip? Write down your ideas.

Daily Schedule
Prepare several possible parent-child "everyday" contact schedules acceptable to you.

Special Days
Prepare a list of the days (holidays) special to you. Define what you mean for each holiday. List several optional schedules for contact with your children on those days.

Extended Vacations
List several vacation contact schedules as options which would be acceptable to you. Include all periods of one week or longer.

2

Co-Parenting I:
The Basics

*Skip this chapter and the next two if you have
no children or if they are over 76 years old.*

LET'S START WITH THE BASICS. Parents who are getting
separated often talk about custody and visitation. Who is in
custody? People in jail, right? Who do you visit? People in the
hospital, the family of the deceased at the mortuary, and your
ancient Aunt Rose who lives a thousand miles away. Most of these
images conjure up pretty negative emotions, right?

When you use the words "custody" and "visitation" with your
partner or with your children, there is an automatic visceral
reaction. Most children over the age of five understand the concept
of custody (prison), and the concept of visiting someone. Visiting
someone is not the same as living with them. Being in custody or
having custody means being controlled or having control, and few
people that I know like being controlled by someone else. The
negative emotional baggage carried by these words and phrases
often makes it very difficult for parents to discuss how they will
take care of their children. The children are often similarly affected
by the use of these words.

So, my first suggestion is to stop using the words "custody" and
"visitation," and start thinking in terms of "co-parenting," "taking
care of the children," or "restructuring the family." I know the last
one is a bit stilted, but that is indeed what you are doing. *The family
continues, even though the adult relationship may end. The two of you
will continue to be Mom and Dad forever; it is only the living
arrangements that need to be adjusted to account for two different
households.*

For some people, co-parenting is a difficult and emotional
subject to discuss. It can be done if you take the time to look at look
at co-parenting as a joint venture. You will need to do a little
resource reading, and be open to options and suggestions that you
might not have thought of on your own. Keep in mind that just

11

because the other parent thought of an idea, doesn't make it automatically bad or unworkable.

If you'd like to do some reading on the topic, a few parenting books I like include: *Mom's House, Dad's House* (I. Ricci), *Parenting After Divorce* (Phil Stahl), and *Sharing Parenthood After Divorce* (C. Ware). You'll find them listed in the Bibliography.

Another important factor to keep in mind when dealing with the issues of co-parenting is that children are not property. You and your partner will continue to be parents to your children for as long as you live. Even though you may not live with your partner, you will probably need to have continued contact regarding your children, especially if the children are very young. Even if they are not young, the children will still need both of you to act as parents and role models, and be sources of love, support, protection, and caring. An antagonistic relationship with the other parent will make it that much more difficult to deal with each other. Don't automatically assume that just because you don't or can't live together, that you can't work together as parents; you can and you must if you are going to be fair to the children. Don't allow yourself to become trapped in a fictional, competitive or antagonistic relationship. Here are some situations that could lead to combative rather than collaborative interactions:

- Each of you may equally want to live with the children.
- One or both of you may feel that if there is no "custody battle" for the children, the children will feel unloved or unwanted. You may also feel that the community will think you are not good parents if you don't "fight" for custody.
- Even if a parent may not want to live with the children, he may feel he needs to fight anyway because of guilt or pressure from family or society.
- One or both parents may cling to the children as a way of clinging to the relationship. ("I've lost my partner and can't bear to lose my children as well.") Such people often put undue pressure on themselves, taking on more and more child-rearing responsibility until they are suffocated. They often try to restrict the children's contact with the other parent and then complain that the other parent never sees the children or takes any parental responsibility.

• One parent may not be able to have the children stay with her because of work or educational demands. (Someone re-entering the workforce or taking courses may need more freedom and flexibility to pursue interviews or do homework.)

There are, of course, other situations and circumstances as well. What is important here is to look at your needs and the needs of the children from an open, honest, and practical standpoint. The hurt, anger, or guilt you may be feeling will recede with time. Even though it is difficult, your thinking needs to be rational and practical rather than emotional at this time. If you become too entrenched in wanting the children for yourself most of the time, consider the following:

How would you feel if your partner saw the children constantly and you had little contact?
For one parent to be with the children constantly may be a disservice to the children, who need both parents, a disservice to the parent who wants more contact, and a disservice to the parent who has the children and needs more time for himself.

The most equitable and healthy arrangement, in most cases, is to share the responsibility for child rearing. Let's look at some of the topics and some alternative ways to handle them. The issues in this chapter and the next are arranged in an order that should make it possible for you to discuss your co-parenting concerns. Follow the order as it is laid out unless some of the issues have already been decided. Do not jump around from issue to issue, as best you can stick with each issue until it is resolved, or until you have gone as far as you can go and need to do more thinking or exploration.

Information Sharing
The issue of sharing information is extremely important for parents. Just how much information sharing goes on varies from couple to couple. Here are some basic areas that are nearly universal:
• How the children are doing in school
• The state of their physical and emotional health
• Any behavioral problems or discipline situations that may be ongoing

The first two issues are rather clear cut, simply requiring that you and your partner discuss how the information sharing will take place, and whether one or both of you will have access to medical and educational information from doctors, schools, hospitals, and other sources. You may both need to sign a statement from the school and doctor's office authorizing each of you to have access to this information.

Somewhat less obvious is the importance for parents to discuss behavioral and disciplinary issues in order to facilitate consistency in child rearing. This does not mean that you, as parents, must have exactly the same rules for behavior at your separate residences. It does suggest that you respect each other's standards, and try to support them with the children. (We will discuss discipline in more detail toward the end of this chapter.) Communication for this support can be developed by regular daily, weekly, or monthly telephone calls, or on an as-needed basis. If you or your partner has "grounded" one of the children for infraction of the rules, it may or may not be appropriate for that child to be grounded when staying with the other parent. Talk over what steps should be taken to support — rather than undermine — the authority of the other parent. Even if you do not agree completely with all of your ex-partner's child-rearing practices, you will find it pays off to reach some agreement on these issues. Remember, you will be looking for support from the other parent, as well.

Educational Information
Do each of you want to have access to educational information about the children? Do you each want to have access to the children's teachers and educational records? Is there any reason why either parent should not have access to the information?

Medical/Health
Do each of you want to have access to medical information about the children? Do you each want to have access to the children's doctors, health professionals, and medical records? Is there any reason why either parent should not have access to the information?

Medical Emergencies

Should each parent be able to sign for emergency medical services for the children in the event of a medical emergency when the children are spending time with that parent? Are there limits to the type of emergency medical services for which a parent may sign? Do you want to be notified, as soon as possible, by the other parent about medical emergencies? What form should notification take? Is there a reason why either parent should not be allowed to sign for emergency medical services for the children?

While it may seem that any child in need of emergency treatment will probably get it, we've all heard of situations where medical services were not provided until the "appropriate parent" was contacted. Clearly this is not always possible (not to mention how disturbing the term "appropriate parent" is!). The entire situation can be handled with a simple permission note or "legal power of attorney" for medical emergencies. You and your partner may wish to furnish each other with written permission allowing either of you to authorize emergency medical services for the children. This is really no different than the form you sign at a daycare center, school or for most team sports, giving the responsible adult permission to sign for emergency medical services if necessary. If you do this, make sure to keep it with you at all times. It won't do you any good to have it and leave it at home.

Miriam and Eli each wanted to have access to information about their children. They agreed that each should have access to teachers, educators and school records. Recognizing that the school was somewhat resistant to sending out duplicate sets of information (while they claimed cost concerns, it seemed they were really trying to avoid getting in the middle of potentially hostile parents), the parents offered a small amount of money to cover the cost of the additional copies and provided self-addressed stamped envelopes so that the teacher and office staff would have a minimal amount of extra work.

With regard to medical information, the parents agreed that both should have access to doctors, health professionals and medical records. They further agreed that any time one parent felt the need to call the doctor's office or took the children to see the doctor for an illness or injury, that they would notify the other parent of the outcome of the call or office visit. Additionally, because of some confusion in the past, they agreed that even if the results from an office visit were negative, that this would be reported to the other parent as well. Finally, the parents agreed that each could sign for emergency medical services for the children, and that any "life-threatening" procedure would be cleared with the other parent if at all possible.

Communication: Parent to Parent

The next issue revolves around how often you want to talk with each other about the children. (I know, you don't really want to talk with them at all!) This is still an issue of information sharing, and has to do with the two of you sharing information with each other, not accessing information from some third party. In situations where the separation has not yet occurred, it may be difficult to estimate how often you want to share information. The question to ask yourself is: How well do we communicate now? If you find that you talk regularly and easily about the children, this may continue without much difficulty. If you find that communication is difficult, and that you avoid talking to each other because of the escalation of hostilities that occurs when you do talk, this may be more of a reason to negotiate a regularly scheduled conversation about the children. The more difficult it is for you to talk, the more likely you will avoid talking to each other, and the more likely the children will suffer from the lack of parental communication and information sharing. Typical phone contact ranges from once or twice a week, to once or twice a month. This does not mean that you cannot talk more often, if necessary. It does imply that you will not talk any less often. The concern is that *if you stop talking, for whatever reason, it will be harder for the two of you to work on parenting issues together.*

Once a frequency is established, the next goal is to select specific days and times that the calls will be made. In this way you will both be less likely to miss the calls, and also less likely to be waiting around for calls that never come. When working on a schedule, try and think in terms of "a window of time." Establishing a specific time, such as 12:00 noon, may be problematic for some people because, if you call at 11:59, you are early and bothering them, and if you call at 12:01, you are late and, "Where the heck were you?" It's more useful to say the call will come "between 12:00 and 1:00." In that way you take into account life's little distractions and interruptions that might interfere with a call at 12:00 sharp. You may also want to discuss which parent will call the other so that there is no confusion. Most parents agree that any conversation of this type will be focused only on the children, and that either parent has the right to disconnect courteously if the conversation strays from parenting issues, or if either party becomes upset with something that has been said.

"Information" includes — but is not limited to — how the children are doing in school, when they become ill or require medical or dental attention, what types of activities they will be involved in, how you can be reached and located in case of emergency. You may wish to have a specific understanding that either of you is free to contact the children's teachers with regard to how they're doing in school and what type of homework help you can give them. Similarly, when the children are expected to be with the one parent for an extended length of time "especially on vacations "basic itineraries are important to share, again in case of emergencies.

Another way to share information is the Children's Data Sheet (see Appendix F). It is a simple useful tool that you can use to share basic, important information.

Communication Between Parents and Children
A related topic is that of communication between a parent and the children when the children are with the other parent. As above, many parents will set up specific schedules for phone contact, while others believe that an open-ended approach is better. Keep in mind that if you use the open-ended approach, you are more likely to be frustrated if you make a call to your children and find that they are not there, or are involved in some project or activity that keeps them from taking your call. All in all, working on communication schedules will help you establish a positive parenting relationship that will aid in the discussion of the other topics to come.

Judy and her husband wanted to make sure to keep abreast of the kids' activities, accomplishments, and developmental changes. When they separated, they decided that they would talk to each other at least once a week to discuss how the children were doing in both households. They agreed that the topic of conversation for this particular weekly phone call would be restricted to issues of the children's development, progress, activities, schedules and schedule changes, and that either parent could discontinue the conversation if he or she became uncomfortable for any reason. They agreed that this weekly phone call would be a minimal contact, fearing that information would be lost if the contact were less frequent. They were free to call each other more often if they had a question however, or if more information was needed to verify something that the children had said. They scheduled the call for Sunday evening, between 9:30 and 10:30 p.m., after the children were put to bed, and to be made by the parent with whom the children were staying that Sunday. If for some reason one parent was going to be unavailable for the phone call, they would notify the other parent, in advance, so that an appropriate alternative time could be selected. At the time of the original negotiations concerning the phone call, they agreed that Sunday could be changed to another day, by mutual consent, if Sunday proved consistently difficult for one of the parents.

Barry and Terry were so angry and so upset they found it difficult to talk at all. After several attempts at sharing information about the children turned into screaming and shouting matches, they agreed that continued interaction at this level would take them in the wrong direction. There were both committed to their children, and recognized the importance of being able to get and give information to the other parent. They decided that until their emotions were in better control, they would share all information in writing. They established a regular pattern of sending notes and sealed letters back and forth with the children to relay information. They later found that using a single, spiral-bound notebook was easier, because all of the information was centrally located and they did not need to continue to look for the scraps of paper containing the information they needed. This writing continued for approximately two years after which time they found it possible to converse in courteous and respectful tones.

Shortly after **Cindy and Doug** separated, Doug was sent to Germany for a two-year change-of-duty station. They recognized that during this time Doug would not get to spend much time with the children. To make matters worse, calls back and forth would be quite expensive. Since they were both computer literate, they agreed to e-mail messages back and forth on a regular basis. They also agreed to obtain scanners so that they could send pictures and documents, copies of the children's homework assignments and grades back and forth with ease. With this setup, Doug could even help with homework using "instant messages." They agreed that when Doug returned to the states, they would re-establish phone contact. They felt that the use of the computers would make their lives easier, and that it would also be good for the children to become more comfortable with the computers in preparation for future school assignments. When Doug found two inexpensive video cameras at the PX, he bought them and sent one home so that video conferencing was also possible.

Daily Schedule

After you have done your reading, the time comes to sit down and discuss schedules. The first is the daily schedule. Focus only on the day-to-day schedule, including weekends, and which of the parents will have contact with and responsibility for which child at what times. A good way to handle this is to set up a calendar-like outline.

Monday	Tuesday	Wednesday	Thursday	Friday	Saturday	Sunday	
							1
							2
							3
							4
							5
							6
							7

Monday through Sunday works best since it is easier to visualize the whole weekend at one glance. Each parent can fill in the blanks according to their preferred schedule for seeing the children. Several outlines may need to be used until a satisfactory schedule is worked out. If you come into the discussion with several schedule options, and your partner does the same, you will find it easier to be open to suggestions and alternatives. These schedule outlines should be done as homework prior to meeting with the other parent, and can then be compared and adjusted as you work together.

One way to set up a schedule is to alternate filling in the calendar spaces until all the blocks are filled in. Days can be broken down into one-half or one-third segments if necessary. Each parent can initial the appropriate blocks, using a pencil so that you can erase and change the schedule as your discussion progresses. (If you or the children have a dry-erase board or chalkboard, it is even easier to do the work). I find using "M's" and "D's" for on Mom and Dad is also a useful way to fill in the blocks. (See example below.)

Monday	Tuesday	Wednesday	Thursday	Friday	Saturday	Sunday	
M	M/D	D/M	D	M/D	M	M	1
M	M	D	D	D/M	D	D	2
M/D	M	D	D/M	M	M	M	3
M	M/D	D/M	D/M	D	D	D	4
							5
							6
							7

Frank and Fanny had been separated for several months before they started working on a separation agreement. They'd had a chance to arrange a contact schedule for their two children that worked for them. Frank traveled out of town a lot in his job, but he still wanted as much contact time with the children as he could manage. The couple didn't want an every-other-weekend schedule; they each wanted time with the children on weekends, and alternating weekends seemed to lack imagination. However, after some discussion, they realized that alternating weekends made the most sense for them because of Frank's travel schedule. They also agreed that Frank would see the children Tuesday evenings on the "off week" (the week which they did not spend the weekend with him). The rest of the time the children stayed with Fanny.

Another way to set up a schedule is to each fill in blocks on your own form for the time that you would like to spend with the children, then overlay the two forms. Where no overlap occurs, the blocks stay. Where there is overlap, you and your partner can negotiate what to do in those blocks of time.

Keep in mind it may take more than one session for you and your partner to reach agreement. This is a point where negotiation and collaboration come into play. Try hard not to stray from the task at hand. Do not drift into other aspects of co-parenting or scheduling; you will cover them later.

When considering day-to-day activities, be sure to discuss and consider what is in the best interests of the children in setting up the schedule. Usually, what is in the best interest of the parents is also in the best interest of the children. A schedule which is too tight and too demanding, requiring one or both of you to run hither and yon, collecting or dropping off children, will probably break down after a short period of time and be non-workable.

Remember also that the children need contact with both of you on a regular and consistent basis.

Bob and Arlene both wanted contact time with the children during the weekend; they also wanted some time to themselves. They set up a four-week rotation, in which the children spent most of the week with Arlene, and saw Bob on Tuesday and Thursday evenings each week. The weekends they handled as follows: the first weekend, Bob picked up the children Friday night, returned them Saturday mid-day, and they spent the rest of the weekend with Arlene. The second weekend they spent entirely with Arlene. On the third weekend they spent Friday evening through Saturday mid-day with Arlene and Saturday mid-day through Sunday evening with Bob. The fourth weekend was spent entirely "Friday through Sunday "with Bob. In this way each parent saw the children three out of the four weekends. Both parents had some time to themselves, either a whole weekend or two parts of a weekend, and were with the children continually for one weekend. They also agreed that weekends could be traded, by mutual agreement, to meet special needs.

Kate and Kevin arranged what amounted to a two-week rotation. Since they lived close to each other "within the same school district "and their housing arrangements allowed, they decided to have equal contact with the children. They set up a schedule in which the children stayed with Kate from Sunday to Saturday, and with Kevin the following Sunday through Saturday. During the "off" week, the children spent one evening with the parent with whom they were not residing.

Debbie and Gary had young children and understood that the children's time frame was different than their own. They wanted to spend equal time with the children and agreed to establish a schedule so that each parent could see the children frequently. They determined it would be possible for the children to be with Debbie on Mondays and Tuesdays, with Gary on Wednesdays and Thursdays, and that they would alternate the weekends. They defined weekends to include the Sunday overnight, so that the weekend parent would drop the children off at day care the following morning. They were able to negotiate this schedule in spite of the fact that they did not communicate well. They each recognized that the other parent had a contribution to make to the welfare of the children by their contact on a regular basis. Because of their animosity toward each other, they agreed that pick-ups and drop-offs would be done at the children's day care.

When I speak of being with the children, I do not necessarily mean 24 hours a day, but rather, having the responsibility for them. Children come and go as schedules and needs decree; parents help them get to and from activities, but are not necessarily with them constantly. When young children are involved you need to consider constant supervision (since leaving them at Wal-Mart would be inappropriate), and make plans for activities, such as going to the park or zoo. Typically, the older children are, the less they want to be with their parents, regardless of whether the parents are living together or apart. This is a normal response in teenagers and should not necessarily be taken as a sign of parental rejection due to separation. When parents set up schedules for older teens, they are often really talking about who will take the children to and from activities, and which parent the children will call when they have questions, need to be picked up, or get in trouble.

Keep in mind also, that who the children stay with should not necessarily be a function of the gender of the parent. That is, girls do not need to spend all of their time with Mom because she has "maternal instincts," nor boys only be with Dad. Decisions ought to be based upon the needs of everyone in the family, both parents must be involved in their children's lives.

> Michael and Lorna decided to use a "nesting" approach to parenting. In "nesting," the children stay in one house and the parents move in and out, according to a prearranged schedule. They agreed to rent an apartment near their house, splitting the cost of rent and utilities for both residences. They established house rules for both residences so that both they and the children would understand each family member's responsibilities.

Daily schedules usually fall into some kind of pattern or cycle, covering a predetermined amount of time. The important thing to remember is not to let the calendar control the schedule. Rather, the schedule should be based upon the needs of the children and parents, and set up accordingly. Generally, schedules don't start anew the first of each month. Rather, they continue on, following the pattern established, until an adjustment is necessary to accommodate the parents' or children's needs or activities.

Most schedules need to have some flexibility. No matter what schedule is selected, someone will miss a transfer time or have to stay late at work or be caught in traffic. Life is not that structured. Make allowances and plan for errors and omissions. *Establish backup plans, safeguard procedures, and people to pick up or care for the children when these typical life events occur.*

Trial Schedules
One of the benefits to negotiating the schedules is that you can try out a schedule to see if it works. This is especially important if you are not yet separated. It is hard for parents who have not been separated to project how a particular schedule will work. Trying out a number of different schedules is a way to determine which works best for your family. Trial schedules are not an option that you will get if you end up the court. Notice that I have been speaking about "schedules that work," not "schedules that you

like." For a schedule to work for a family does not necessarily mean that everyone will be in love with it. Rather, it means that everyone can live with it and that it makes sense.

Additionally, as children grow older their needs change, and there is a likelihood that the schedule will need to be adjusted as well. Some parents develop a secondary schedule that will accommodate co-parenting as the children reach certain ages or educational milestones. Others choose to renegotiate the scheduling needs annually or when the children reach a certain age (see renegotiation).

Adam and Aileen were not separated when they started negotiating the parenting plan. They developed three schedules that they thought had potential. They agreed to try schedule A and, if both were not satisfied after three months, to try schedule B. If they were not satisfied with B after three months, they would move to schedule C. If that didn't work, they agreed to renegotiate the contact arrangement. The ability to run trial schedules and renegotiate was important to them because they did not know how the schedules they had projected on paper would actually work out. Because Adam and Aileen had very young children, they also agreed, regardless of which schedule they adopted, to re-discuss and perhaps renegotiate the schedule every two years.

Schedules do not need to be the same for all children. In some cases it may be appropriate for parents to split up the children, either on a regular basis or on a periodic basis, in order to focus more attention on a particular child or to accommodate a particular child's needs or interests.

Sharla and Bruce arranged their parenting schedule so that four of their five children would be with Bruce on Tuesday and Thursday evening. This gave Sharla the opportunity to take daughter Leah to karate class, an activity they both enjoyed.

Sue and Bill recognized they wanted to spend some one-on-one time with each of their children. They felt it would be good both for the children and them. They arranged a schedule in which the children would spend some time together with each parent, and other times when the children would spend individual time with each parent. In this way each child would get individual attention and still have time with parents and siblings in a more complete family constellation.

There are almost as many different parenting arrangements as there are families. The critical element here is to figure out a way that the two of you can work together to take care of the children now, and make any necessary adjustments in the future. *The greater the level of collaboration, the greater the likelihood of raising normal, healthy kids.*

Special Days
The next discussion involves scheduling for holidays and "special days." Prior to your meeting, develop a list of the holidays and special days that you would like to discuss. Talk about who will have contact with the children on religious and national holidays such as Christmas, Easter, Yom Kippur, Rosh Hashanah, Thanksgiving, Fourth of July, Memorial Day, and Labor Day. Be sure to also plan for children's birthdays, parents' birthdays, grandparents' birthdays, Mother's Day, and Father's Day. Any other days that are special to the family "or you would like to make special "should also be considered.

"Holidays" may be *defined* in different ways. For example, Thanksgiving may be thought of as Thursday only. In most school districts, children have Friday off from school as well, so some families define Thanksgiving as Thursday and Friday. Some folks define Thanksgiving as Thursday, Friday, Saturday, Sunday (giving families the opportunity to go "over the river and through the woods" to grandmother's house for turkey and pumpkin pie).

There is no right answer in defining a particular holiday, but it is important for both of you to come to an understanding ahead of time. This will help avoid confusion and conflict in the future.

In addition to how a holiday is *defined*, is the question of how the holiday will be *handled*. There are several options to consider:

• The same parent has the children for the same holiday year after year.

• The parents alternate the holiday each year.

• The parents split the holiday in some fashion each year (mornings with Mom and afternoons with Dad the first year; mornings with Dad and afternoons with Mom the second year).

• The parents can celebrate the holiday together with the children.

• The parents can negotiate each year how the holiday will be handled.

This last is the shakiest because if you cannot agree to an outcome, it will only cause additional conflict and hard feelings. Rather, it makes more sense to select one of the other options above for each holiday. Then, in any given year, you can negotiate some other way to handle that holiday, with the understanding that if you cannot reach agreement, you will use the written document as your safety net.

> David and Sheila developed a list of special days for their family, then agreed to alternate holidays each year. In the "odd" years the children were with David for Thanksgiving (Thursday, Friday, Saturday and Sunday), and Christmas Day, and with Sheila for Christmas Eve (they were careful to define Christmas Eve as including the overnight) and Easter (defined as spring break). In the "even" years they would be with David for Christmas Eve and Easter, and with Sheila on Thanksgiving and Christmas Day.

When you get together combine your lists and work through the special days one at a time. Start with something easy like Mother's Day, Father's Day, or your birthday. Stick with each holiday until you have an agreement on how it will be handled.

Michael and Sandy, in addition to deciding some of the already important special days for their family, took the opportunity to set aside some other days "which had not been so special in the past" in order to develop new family traditions. The couple agreed that Michael would spend time with the children on the Fourth of July, and Sandy would spend time on the long Presidents' Day weekend in February. These days had never been special to the family in the past, but would be in the future, since they now represented additional opportunities to share time with the children.

Richard and Linda decided to take advantage of the fact that Rosh Hashanah, Yom Kippur and Hanukkah could be celebrated on multiple days. They agreed that Richard would have the first night of Rosh Hashanah and the day of Yom Kippur, while Linda would have the first night of Yom Kippur and the second night of Rosh Hashanah. They further agreed to alternate these each year. For Chanukah they agreed to split the eight nights equally each year. They agreed to negotiate who would get which nights, three weeks before Chanukah began each year.

Additionally, they had to decide how to deal with childcare responsibilities for winter and spring break when the children were off from school. They decided to try to take some of their vacation time during these periods, and also arranged for day care coverage. They asked the parents of their children's friends to act as a backup in case of an emergency.

As with the day-to-day activities, there are many factors to be considered in planning for holidays. The children may have desires and ideas about what will happen on various special days. The older the children, the more independent they become. There is a greater need to be with peers, and a desire to spend less time with their parents. (I know it's hard to believe your 11-year-old wouldn't want to spend every waking minute with you, but it is true!) As with other parenting issues, Mom and Dad will make the final decision, however, be sure to consider the children's developmental needs and interests. As the children get older certain variations or allowances will, in all likelihood, need to be made. You may wish to agree to renegotiate the special days and special holidays at various future milestones.

Before moving on, I want to remind you about family reunions and grandparents' birthday. These events are often overlooked. Especially for elder, frail family members who may not be around for many more years, these occasions are very special. It is important for all family members that prior contacts and bonds are maintained. Take the time to consider how these occasions can be celebrated.

Extended Vacations
Extended periods of time in which the children are off from school generally include summer vacations, winter vacations, and sometimes spring vacations.

> **Gertrude and Bob** had always spent summer vacation at the beach, renting a small cottage near relatives and friends. Even while separated they felt it was important, while the children were young, to continue to provide the experience of the familial and recreational setting during the summer. They agreed to continue to rent the cottage and to split the time with the children by alternating two-week blocks of time. They arranged for neighbors and relatives to provide day care for the children while they were at work, and returned every evening to be with the children.

You will want to consider any special daily scheduling or day care that will need to be arranged while the children are out of school. Additionally, extended contact time for each of the parents may need to be discussed. For example, a parent may want to go away on vacation with the children for a week or two. Is it all right for the children to go along? If so, for how long? How far in advance should you plan? Should specific blocks of time be set aside to which each parent is obligated? You will want to discuss your own needs with regard to activities, work and vacation, and how arrangements can be handled to suit the needs of you and your children. You will want to discuss these issues now, even if you do not have much vacation time coming from your current work (or the funds to go on vacation even if you have a time). Look to the future. Take advantage of the fact that you are working well together now. It may not always be this way.

Susan and Jack had to work at jobs that did not provide much flexibility in time. They did agree that the children could be sent to one-week of summer camp. They further agreed that each parent could take the children for one week to share their vacation. They agreed that specific times for the vacations would be decided in a discussion before the end of school each year. The rest of the summer would be handled according to the daily schedule that they had previously set up. Each parent helped make arrangements for day care for the youngest child, and planned daily activities to keep the older children busy and out of harm's way.

Issues you will want to discuss include: the children going to summer camp, visiting relatives, going off with friends or by themselves for periods of time.

Judy and Dave each had two weeks of vacation during the summer. They recognized, however, that they might not want to spend all of their vacation time with their children. They worked out an arrangement that provided each parent one week of vacation with the children, and a second week without the children. The scheduling decisions would be made before May 1st of each year. During the week each was away on vacation without the children, the other parent was responsible for the entire week of childcare.

It is generally understood that *holidays and vacations will supersede the daily schedule, but vacations will not supersede the holiday schedule*. What this means is that if it is your weekend and the other parent's holiday, they will get the holiday (or vice-versa). It also means that neither of you can take your vacation on the other parent's holiday and wipe out that holiday. It can, of course, be done by mutual agreement, but not unilaterally. As with everything else, vacation agreements should be clear, concise, and understood by both. Don't forget to write down what is decided, so there will be no confusion later.

If you and/or your spouse have trouble with any of the material in this chapter, please consult a professional mediator.

"Home Work" for the Co-Parenting II Discussion

It helps to have both parents complete each assignment in writing prior to the discussion and to bring the written work to the session. When several items are suggested, prepare two or more variations (options) for discussion.

Reading. Read this "Co-Parenting II" chapter before completing the following assignments. Read and follow the Agenda for this topic provided in Appendix A.

Relatives and Others. List people with whom the children may and may not have contact. How will you control contact? Write down some options.

Transportation. How will transportation be handled? Will it be shared, or is one person primarily responsible?

Sick Children. Who will care for the children? Who will take time off from work? Will the children go back and forth between homes if they are sick?

Extra-Curricular Activities. How will each parent participate in, provide transportation for, and/or support the children's after-school activities, sports, music, etc.? Who decides what activities the children can participate in?

Gifts, Clothing, Allowance. Who decides? Who pays? Can you cooperate in allowing the children to make decisions in these areas when appropriate?

Moving. Specify what a "move" means to you (time, distance, other factors). Prepare several alternate contact schedules for dealing with potential moves.

Changes in Jobs, Residence, Marital Status. Recognize that your lives will change in the future. How will your parenting plan adjust to these changes?

3

Co-Parenting II:
"Fine Tuning"

RELATIVES AND OTHERS

So far we have dealt with sharing information, dealing with medical emergencies, communication, day-to-day activities, the contact that each parent wishes to have with the children, special days, and extended vacations. Another area of consideration is who else will have access to and contact with the children.

There are other people, such as grandparents, aunts and uncles, cousins and friends who want and deserve contact with your children. They may have formed close relationships that could prove to be beneficial to the children. In addition, the children may be used to spending time with the family and friends and may wish for these relationships to continue. You will want to discuss your desire as to whether or not such visits should continue.

> For **Molly and Adrian,** deciding about contact with relatives was quite easy. Their parents were relatively young and had had quite a bit of contact with the children in the past. Neither Molly nor Adrian had any problems with their children seeing grandma and grandpa from either side of the family. They both agreed that the children could not only visit the grandparents, they could also stay overnight when invited.

Keep in mind, regardless of how you feel about your in-laws (or your own family), if they have had a close relationship with your children, they may provide a stabilizing factor for the children. If the contact has been frequent and is abruptly discontinued, this is another potentially traumatic loss which your children will have to overcome.

Miriam's parents were quite old and a little senile. While they loved the grandchildren, they were not capable of taking care of them by themselves. Miriam and Eli agreed that while either parent could take the children to visit Miriam's parents, the children would not be able to stay there without some responsible adult present. In order not to cause a family squabble or insult Miriam's parents, they also agreed that, for the time being, the children should not be left unattended with Eli's parents, either. They acknowledged, between themselves, that at some later time, it might be appropriate for the children to spend time unattended with Eli's parents.

Death of a Parent

It will be useful for the two of you to discuss what will happen if one of you should die. The first issue is what will happen to the children? Where will they reside and who will care for them? Will they go to the other parent full-time? In most cases the answer is "yes." However, there are situations where other arrangements make more sense. If the children are to live with someone other than the biological parent, it will be important to talk with that other person to verify that they agree to accept that responsibility. You may even need to draw a separate agreement to make sure this will be accomplished. Do not be distracted by financial, insurance, or other issues; they will be covered later in this book.

Rachel and Andy never saw much of each other. Andy was always at work and never spent much time with the children. They discussed and agreed that if Rachel died, the children would live primarily with her sister Halley, and that Andy would continue with the same contact schedule that he and Rachel had worked out. They also agreed that if Andy's job changed, resulting in less traveling and more time locally, he and Halley would negotiate a new daily schedule. Halley was, of course, contacted prior to putting her name in the agreement. She agreed to take the children if necessary. Since Andy and Halley got along reasonably well, both parents were comfortable with this plan.

The second issue is whether the surviving parent will encourage and assist the children in having a relationship with the deceased parent's family. Is this something you would like to have done? Is this something that you and the other parent can agree to? It is often very reassuring to know that the other parent will support the children's relationship with relatives on your side of the family.

Sam and Clair felt that family bonds and relationships were very important. They agreed that, even though they did not get along very well with their in-laws, in the event of the death of one parent, the other parent would continue to make sure the children had contact with the deceased parent's family.

Transportation

Transportation is more than just a question of how the children get back and forth from one parent's home to the other. Also included are how they get to school, to after-school activities, to sports and games, to work, and to social activities (for example, dates). For many parents, transportation is just a pain in the butt. They don't want to do any more than necessary. For other parents, it is a punishment for the breakup of the relationship. ("You want them? You come and get them.) And for others it is seen as an opportunity to interact and learn from and about them. (My wife insists that she can learn more about what is going on with our children in a 15-minute carpool trip with their friends than a 45-minute inquisition under a hot spotlight.) Regardless of how you view it, transporting your children is part of parenting. The question is, who will do what? This may be partially affected by the number of children and the kind of vehicle you drive. If one of you has a van, and the other a two-seater Corvette, part of your transportation responsibilities may be preordained (unless you are willing to swap cars occasionally, or each has a vehicle that accommodates the crew).

Rachel and David realized that the outcome of transportation was a foregone conclusion. David lived two hours away and came up only on weekends to see the children. They agreed that Rachel would drive the children to their various activities during the week when they lived primarily with her, and David would drive them to games, parties, and other activities that came up on the weekend. Both realized that there would be some "dead time," and recognized that even though Dad had driven two hours to be with the children, he couldn't expect them spend 100 percent of the weekend with him. His status as a parent-driver didn't change because he lived two hours away.

Jack and Esther treated the situation this way: Each would drive the children wherever they (the children) needed to be during their designated time with the children, and each would pick the children up from the other when their designated time began. In that way, each was motivated to be on time in order to maximize the amount of time with the children. Additionally, by picking up the children from the other parent, they were actively doing something positive, rather than passively sitting around and getting angry when the other parent was late bringing the children back.

Sol and Andrea both traveled a lot in their work. They agreed that they would try to cover for each other when one was not available. They discussed itineraries each week and shared schedules and calendars. They also established a large safety net of friends and family who could or would be available if neither parent could transport the children. They agreed that cell phones made sense, and built the cost into their budgets so that each would be as accessible as possible in case of last-minute arrangements.

Sick Children

One of the areas often overlooked by parents developing a parenting plan is the issue of how to care for sick children. When I say "how to care," I am really talking about two different levels. Level one revolves around when it is appropriate to take the children to see a health-care professional; level two addresses which parent will take the time (from work?) to be with the sick children. At level one, some parents will want to discuss and decide when it is appropriate — or not necessary — to take the children to a health-care professional. Are there certain signs and symptoms that warrant a visit to the doctor? This is especially important when a child has a history of illness and one of the parents has not been that involved in the medical care of the child. Examples include asthma, allergies, diabetes, and emotional problems.

Rose had spent more time with their asthmatic child (and had asthma herself) than Jules, so she and Jules devoted a fair amount of time talking about the symptoms and precursor signs of an asthma attack. They agreed that Jules would take a short course at the "asthma foundation" so that he might better understand and be prepared for any asthmatic situation that might arise. He was, of course, not ignorant about the condition, since he had been helping Rose for 10 years. He attended the class to maximize his knowledge, protect his child, and reassure Rose, who was hesitant about the child spending overnights with him.

Tobi was a bit of a hypochondriac. Even she admitted it. Historically, she had taken the children to the pediatrician for simple coughs and sneezes on multiple occasions. She and Ian discussed and agreed that, except in an emergency, she would call the clinic first to talk to the P.A. or nurse practitioner, discuss the situation, and be guided by what they said.

Ian was just the opposite. He almost never went to the doctor and seldom took the children, sometimes even when he should have. He agreed that he too would take temperatures more frequently, check symptoms, and that he would check with the staff at the doctor's office and be guided by their suggestions.

The second set of issues has to do with who will care for the children when they are too sick to be in school. Who will take time off from work? Will the children be transferred back and forth, as per the daily schedule? Who should the school call if the children get sick at school? Will the sick child be separated from the healthy children, or will they go back and forth together? Will a sick child keep the same contact schedule?

Barry and Cindy recognized that Barry had a weak stomach. Every time one of the five children started vomiting, if Barry was around, he vomited, too. They agreed that if the children had the flu with an upset stomach Cindy would care for the children. If there were other problems, bumps, bruises, or headaches, he would make himself available to nurture the sick children. They also agreed to have the school call Cindy first so she could screen the illness and assess whether she or Barry would take over.

Suzanne and Bill agreed to take turns caring for sick children and taking time off from work. Additionally, they agreed that the sick children would follow the daily schedule, unless medically contraindicated by a physician.

Extracurricular Activities

One of the concerns that some parents share in mediation is that children are enrolled in various activities without the consent of the other parent. Not only is this discourteous, it often leads to lack of support for the child's activity by the parent who has had no input. One of the greatest concerns for this unilateral decision-making about activities is that the child who is involved in these activities has less time to spend with the other parent. Some parents come to feel that to sign up for these activities is a purposeful attempt on the part of the other parent to limit contact or to relegate the parent to status of chauffeur. (I have nothing against chauffeurs!)

There are several issues that need to be considered here. The first is who can sign up children for extracurricular activities? Are they are any activities in which the children should not be enrolled? (Karate? Skydiving?) Who will be responsible for transportation of the children to these activities? And, of course, how are these extracurricular activities paid for? On the other side of the coin, should you restrict your child's activities just because you don't feel like driving? And, once signed up, should children be allowed to avoid activities by using the other parent as an excuse either on a periodic basis — "I don't want ago to the game today" — or on a continual basis — "I don't want to sign up for dance class, because then there won't be enough time for Dad to take me shopping after dinner." There is also the question of whether children should be allowed to resign from an activity, mid-course, if they don't like something about it. As children get older they are often involved more with activities and friends than they are with their parents. This is a natural and normal outgrowth of their social and skills development phase.

Gifts

Many parents want to discuss how and what gifts will be purchased for the children. There is a concern, and sometimes a history, of one parent providing bigger, brighter, more expensive presents for the children than the other parent is able to match. This sometimes turns into a competition, and other times may result in children indicating a dissatisfaction with the parent who is not able to compete in the gift-giving games. In some families, gifts are given as a way to purchase affections. In other situations, they may be used as a way to make up for missed time with a child. In addition to special occasions, gifts are given whenever the parent sees the child. Gifts are not always given as a way to buy affection, or assuage guilt; some people really enjoy giving gifts, and have the capability of doing so. Gift-giving concerns may also exist for grandparents, aunts. uncles, and others.

Some parents will agree in advance to be careful and even to coordinate the gifts that they give, so as not to duplicate nor set up a competition between the parents. Some parents will put maximum dollar amounts that they will spend on gifts, and some will agree to speak with family members so that gift giving does not get out of hand. In some cases the parents will agree to give gifts together (coming from both parents), in order to minimize the concerns about competition and ability to pay.

Clothing

The purchase of clothing is a financial issue that will be addressed later on. This section will focus on the (mostly) non-financial issues. Some common clothing concerns are:

- whether or not the children will have clothing in both households.
- whether they will take clothing back and forth between households.
- who will wash the clothing and when and how it will be returned.

One of the ways that you can be sure the children feel up part of both households is to make sure that they have basic supplies, including clothing, in both locations. The more "stuff" that a child has to take back and forth, the more they feel like a guest or a visitor, rather than a member of the household. It is not possible, however, for most families to have a complete set of clothes to accommodate all seasons and activities in each household. What can you do? If a child does bring clothing with them, should they take it back with them? What if they've been wearing it all day and it's dirty? What if they forget something? You will want to spend some time discussing these issues with the other parent. Typically, one parent in a household generally purchases most of the clothing for the children (standard division of labor) and the other has little understanding of cost (it's always too much), style (what's in this week will surely change next week), and size. Many parents will agree to share the responsibility and cost of the children's clothes. In this way they become more aware of what's going on with their children, and have a far greater appreciation — or despair — of their children's clothing needs, values, and interests.

Marcy and Dave had always disagreed about their children's clothing. Marcy always complained about needing more money to buy clothes for the children, and Dave frequently made comments about going to the poor house. Both were concerned about the other's concerns and approaches to clothing, therefore, they agreed to get together three times a year for major seasonal clothing purchases. This way they could be reassured that each would be in agreement with the purchases, and understand the costs were real, not inflated.

Elyse told her parents that they were crazy if they thought she was going to wear tennis shoes from K-Mart. They explained that their budget would not support the lifestyle and standard of living that she aspired to, in order to look like her friends. They agreed that she could have more expensive clothing if she would contribute to the purchase by working, so she established a baby sitting service.

Trish and Patrick didn't have much money. They had four children — two in their teens — and all four were interested in looking good and dressing as well as their friends. Since they knew clothing would be an issue, Trish and Patrick asked their large families to give gifts of clothing at the various gift-giving occasions. Their families agreed to help any way they could, and were given lists of clothing that the children wanted. In this way the clothing expense was reduced, and they could use their funds for other important purposes.

Allowance

Allowance is another financial issue that has implications for competition. Many parents want an understanding concerning who will be responsible for paying allowance, how much the allowance will be, and making sure that the children do not do any "double dipping" by getting allowance twice.

Sally and Rob wanted to make sure that they were perceived equally as providers. They agreed that when it came time to pay allowance to the children, they would alternate weeks. In order to accomplish this in a structured way, and since they had the children on alternating weekends, they agreed that allowances would be paid on Saturday by the parent with whom the children were staying. They also agreed how much the allowance would be for each child.

Forgetting Stuff at the Other Parent's House

One of the issues that upsets parents is when the child or the other parent forgets something that belongs to the child and leaves it behind. It is inevitable that this will happen; we all forget things. Sometimes it is clothing, other times a toy, sports equipment, musical instrument, or a school book. How this is handled will, in some ways, depend on how far apart the parents live from each other. If the parents live close, the hassle is quite minimal. If the parents live some distance, it can be a problem, especially when the object left behind is needed by the child to function in the coming days. A couple of options: doing without the item; having the parent that forgot the item return it; or having the parent that wants the item (on behalf of the child?) go get it. This is another area that can result in competition and get out of hand if it is not handled carefully. It is also an area that, depending on the age of the child, can be made into a learning experience by establishing levels of responsibility. What's important here is to understand the potential disruption caused by leaving something behind. The schoolbook or musical instrument are hard to replace, though not impossible if one is creative. Perhaps the pages of homework out of a book could be scanned and sent to another computer. With a little forethought you might be able to borrow another instrument from a household where the child is no longer using it, and keep an instrument in each household.

Making a list of items taken to make sure everything is returned can be a big help in these situations.

Moving

What will happen if one parent wants or needs to leave the area? How will co-parenting activities continue? How will leaving the area change each parent's schedule of contact with the children? How does one define "moving"? For some couples "moving" means leaving the community; for others it means leaving the county or state. Some measure moving in terms of miles, minutes, or hours from the other parent's home. You will probably find the last to be the most useful definition. It is easy to see that parents could live in different counties or different school districts, and literally live right next door to each other. Clearly this would not interfere with their parenting. The difficulty arises when parents live so far apart that they cannot easily and consistently live up to the parenting plan that they have established. The question becomes: "If I have to drive 45 minutes (or 60, 70, etc.) longer than I usually do to pick up the kids, and then take them back to my apartment, is that a reasonable thing to do, and will it leave any time for me and the kids?" *The key to developing a successful parenting plan is that the plan needs to be realistic. That is, each parent must be able to live up to the plan on a consistent and dependable basis.*

> When **Bill and Veronica** separated, they were pretty sure that moving was not going to be a very big issue. Each of them had secure jobs that did not require travel, and most of their family was located nearby. They decided that if a move by either of them required travel of more than an hour (one way by car), this would be reason to re-evaluate and, if necessary, renegotiate the contact schedule with the children.

When parents do move a significant distance from each other, they will need to decide where and with which parent the children will spend most of their time. Should it be in the old community with the parent who stays behind, or in a new community with the parent who moves? Some couples feel that the marital breakup is traumatic enough for the children, and that moving the children (especially children in school) puts too much additional strain on them. Others feel that moving is not automatically detrimental to the children, and should be considered on a case-by-case basis, taking into consideration the children's emotional wellbeing, how they are dealing with the separation, and how they are dealing with each parent.

Will and Trudy had a unique situation. Not only did Will's job require that he travel quite a bit, there was a good chance that Trudy was going to be offered a promotion that might require her to relocate. The couple agreed that if either of them had to move (defined by them as more than 50 miles one way), the other would make every attempt to relocate in the same area and to continue their co-parenting schedule. They agreed to keep each other apprised of any potential moves so that the other could explore the possibility of a move as well. They agreed to renegotiate the schedule if mutual relocation was not possible.

If a move is probable, you may want to make a note to discuss any potential change in financial arrangement brought about by relocation. Don't discuss it now! Come back to it when you get to "Support," chapter 4. The main question is how expenses for the children's travel between parental homes will be handled. This is especially important if public transportation is to be used. For now you can address how transportation needs are to be met. Will you share the transportation costs and responsibilities? Will each parent drive one way? Will you meet in the middle and transfer the child, so that each leg of the trip will not be too long? If public transportation will be used, what form? Will the parents accompany the children, or will they travel alone? What other resources exist for helping with transportation? (Example: Is there a college nearby with students who might also be traveling at the same time?) These are important issues to discuss, at least philosophically, even if you are not planning a move.

Don't be fooled or lulled into a false sense of security about moving just because you have a good job or your parents are near. If someone makes you an offer too good to pass up, if you win the lottery, or if your new (as-yet unfound) love's main mansion is located three states away, you might consider a move. If your employer is taken over by "Gigantic Corporation," and you are given a new department to head at triple the salary in a new location, you might want to think about a move and what it could provide for your children. One never knows what will happen to us in our lifetime. Don't agree? Did you think this would happen?

Ellen and Larry's situation was very uncertain. Ellen was out job hunting and had several tentative offers, varying from a local job with a modest income, to a job with intermediate income about one-and-a-half hours away, to a really good job with a high-level income about four hours away. The couple came up with several contact schedules that provided for the children to spend more and more time with Larry as Ellen moved farther and farther from their home ground. The choice was up to Ellen as to which job to select. The agreement was that Ellen got to choose which job she wanted, and they would try the new schedule. If the new schedule did not work, the parents would reevaluate and renegotiate after a trial period of six months.

Change in Residence

Like "moving" some parents will agree to reevaluate and, if necessary, renegotiate the parenting plan if either parent changes residence (even if it is with in the defined area). The considerations for a new residence include the potential for making new friends, engaging in new activities (or old activities in new places), and being exposed to a different environment.

Change in Jobs

A job change for the parents may affect their ability to spend time with the children (daily, holiday, or vacation schedule). The times they have to go to work or come back from work may affect their ability to get the kids up in the morning, get them to school, pick them up after school, or get them to or from after-school activities. New jobs often add additional stress and pressure to the individual and to the family. Some parents agree that if a job change occurs for one parent, the other parent will take the children more frequently for a short period of time in order to allow the parent with the new job to acclimate. (This can also be helpful in a job search situation.)

Sometimes a job change means a change in location, as well. In our present and very-mobile society, it is not unusual for people to be transferred within an organization to different geographical locations. In some situations people are offered jobs in different parts of the country.

Emmanuel was an airline pilot who had been told to expect a transfer to a new "hub" within the next 18 months. The move represented advancement in seniority and income. He and his wife, Meg, recognized that this increase in income would help the family. Meg agreed since she had no familial ties in this area and no significant other in her life at the present, that she would attempt to move to the same location as Emmanuel, given enough prior notice. Meg recognized that she was not being forced to make the move, and that the children would benefit from having access to both parents. The parents agreed that the move on Meg's part was voluntary, and that if something occurred between the time of this agreement and when the move actually took place, Meg could decline the move and they would renegotiate based on their different geographical areas and new salaries.

In some cases, all that can be done is to re-evaluate and renegotiate based on new locations. In other cases, it may be possible for the other parent to relocate as well.

John and Martha agreed that it was important for their children to have contact with both parents. This did not change when Martha was transferred to the Midwest from their home on the East Coast. Both agreed that regular phone calls were not enough, and that they would like the children to spend time with each of them whenever possible. Since a home base for school was necessary, they agreed that the children would spend most of the school year with John. The rest of the time, one weekend per month, most holidays, and most of the summer would be spent with Martha. Where transportation back and forth was necessary, the parents agreed to share the cost proportional to income. When public transportation was used, the parents made arrangements with the local university by advertising in the school newspaper to hire the services of students who were traveling to supervise and oversee the children during their travel. Since the schedule was planned fairly far in advance, they had time to screen applicants and make appropriate selections. This also provided time for the children to get to know the students prior to travel time, allowing everyone to feel more comfortable.

Change in Marital Status

This is obviously a difficult issue for some people. Keep in mind that the phrase "marital status" includes significant others (serious dating) as well. One of the most common issues that arises is how much, if any, should the children have contact with the new "friend." Often, especially in the early stages of separation when parents and children are the most fragile, there is a hesitancy or resistance for one parent to allow the children to spend time with the other parent and their significant other. On the one hand, there is some research and opinion that suggests too many changes in a child's life during the early stages of their parents' separation is not healthy. On the other hand, the concern about the children's well-being as it relates to the other parent's friend seems to fade when both parents have friends. It is not my task here to write a chapter on the pros and cons of dating and marriage after separation and divorce. If you are seeing someone, or thinking about seeing someone, now would be a good time to read some of the books dealing with children, divorce, and dating.

At some point in time there is a pretty good likelihood that one or both of you will indeed have new partners. (I know, you say now, "I'll never do it again." Almost everyone says that. You mean it now; you may change your mind later on — or tomorrow. Most people do). The questions that arise include: Who is able to transport the kids? Who is able to establish rules and discipline? Who is able to enroll the children in activities and make decisions? Most parents will find it useful to discuss these issues at separation or divorce.

Sandy and Doug had been separated for over four years. Each was "seeing" someone else they intended to marry after the divorce. Each spent quite a bit of time with their significant other, and they all often found themselves standing on the sidelines at one sports event or another. Their new partners had, on occasion, taken the children to certain activities when they were not available. When they recognized that this was likely to be a permanent arrangement, the four adults sat down and established a set of ground rules for dealing with Sandy and Doug's children. They discussed and agreed that Sandy and Doug would be the final "deciders" for major child-rearing decisions. They also agreed that either of the new partners could be involved with setting house rules and providing discipline and structure, within the bounds of what they knew to be acceptable to Sandy and Doug. They agreed to have periodic meetings to discuss how things were going, and to try to avoid letting any small disagreements fester into large ones.

These are all questions that will be useful to address now, even if there is no one special in your life right now. Remember, one of our basic philosophies is to look to the future. If either of you remarries, what will be the role of the stepparent? Will you sit down and talk with the children in a team effort for parenting? *Try not to look at the step-parent as a threat.* Rather, consider them an ally and — even better — another set of wheels to take your children where they need to go.

Jane and Tad took a different approach. They established a "hands-off" philosophy. They agreed that each parent was free to establish household procedures and discipline. They agreed that they trusted each other's judgment (including choice of new partners), and that they did not particularly want to deal with each other's new partners. They agreed that all communication would be kept between the two of them, and that, exclusive of emergencies, they would stick to their regularly-scheduled phone calls and renegotiation activities.

Different still was the approach of **Susan and Jack.** They agreed initially that neither would spend time with their significant other when the children were spending time with them. That is, within the bounds of the daily and holiday schedule, they agreed that if the children were spending time with either parent, that parent would not have their significant other spend much time at their residence, nor have the significant other spend the night, even if the children were already in bed. They agreed that this would continue until both parents were sure that the children had adjusted to the separation. They could not plan on how long this would take, so they set a minimum of six months so that they would not feel unduly pressured to make a decision in this regard.

If you and/or your spouse have trouble with any of the material in this chapter, please consult a professional mediator.

"Home Work" for the Co-Parenting Discussion

It helps to have both parents complete each assignment in writing prior to the discussion and to bring the written work to the session. When several items are suggested, prepare two or more variations (options) for discussion.

Reading. Read this "Co-Parenting III" chapter before completing the following assignments. Read and follow the Agenda for this topic provided in Appendix A.

Discipline and House Rules. Your children will be living part-time in two households. Will the rules for them be consistent enough to avoid confusion and insecurity?

Decisions, and Tie-Breakers. If mutual decision making will be used by the parents, what will happen in the event of a tie? What other people would both of you consider to help in the decision-making process?

Custody. Consider how decision making will take place in each major area of child rearing: religion, education, medical treatment, behavior standards and social interaction. Can you make any prior agreements (e.g., religion, education)?

4

Co-Parenting III:
Custody and Other Key Decisions

R ENEGOTIATION

Nothing ever stays the same. We change, our needs change, our interests and activities change. The same is true of our children. Unless you are establishing schedules and guidelines for a 17-year-old, the chances are that you will want to consider handling things differently as the children get older. Unfortunately, many people don't like change. Some people say, "Now that I have negotiated this plan I intend to stick with it, and I intend for you to stick with it. Let's not muck it up by continually changing it." I agree that continual changes, especially the unilateral kind will often cause problems with a parenting plan. I also recognize that *there is a need for flexibility, since no schedule will work on an absolute basis.* Life is too fraught with glitches for a schedule to work exactly. Therefore, now would be a good time to incorporate an acknowledgment and understanding that there may be a need for a parenting plan adjustment in the future. Now would also be a good time to discuss the renegotiation schedule. By agreeing to a renegotiation schedule you (or your partner) are not agreeing to change, only to discuss the possibility of change. Some parents want to evaluate the parenting plan and discuss possible adjustments every six months, others once a year, and still others, every two years. Some families choose anniversaries, such as the child's fifth, tenth, and fifteenth birthdays, while others select milestones, such as entering elementary school, middle school, and high school.

Quinn and Robin understood that having young children would require constant adjustment on their part for a long time to come. They agreed to evaluate the parenting plan six months after the separation, allowing them to make necessary adjustments after things had settled down a bit. They agreed to reevaluate and, if necessary, renegotiate the parenting plan each year thereafter. They established a "drop-dead date" of July 15th each year. They agreed that if neither had a concern about the parenting plan, they need not meet, and that if either did have a concern, they would discuss it before July 15th. They chose this summer deadline so that they could project future needs and changes as the children went into the new school year. They recognized that if they waited till the end of summer, they might not have enough time before school started to make the necessary adjustments.

Art and Sarah Jane agreed to reevaluate the parenting plan on an annual basis. They initially decided to use the date of their separation as the time when they would meet. As the time for the first meeting approached, they recognized a growing discomfort that they attributed to the anniversary of the separation. They agreed to change the meeting to another date that would not have such negative memories and emotions.

Discipline and House Rules

One of the questions that often comes up is how discipline will be handled in two households. Parents often do not always have the same values, child-rearing philosophies, or approaches to discipline. This is true whether they are living together or apart. While together, they usually either moderate their views and approaches to accommodate the other parent, or one parent does most of the discipline ("Just wait until your father gets home"). In many cases, parents have different views on discipline, starting when their child is very young.

Now that separation has occurred and the parents are living apart, they are (or see themselves) freer to "raise the children as I think they should have been raised all along." In a few cases this can lead to pretty diverse views. More often, however, the parties understand the importance of consistency in child rearing and agree to work together to provide the needed consistency.

"Discipline" and "house rules" are two areas that require discussion. "House rules" are just that – rules or guidelines that parents use to give guidance to children and establish expectations for their behavior. Examples include: household chores, homework, laundry, bath schedules (if they are teenagers – trying to keep them out of the bathroom; if they are pre-teens trying to get them into the bathroom), acceptable language, driving, and dating rules. "Discipline" is what is required when children don't comply with house rules.

The questions that arise from these issues revolve around whether there will be house rules; if so, will they be the same in both households? Will they be posted (written up and displayed) so there will be less confusion? If they are different for each household, will they be shared with the other parent? How often will they be adjusted, amended, or expanded? Additionally, and very importantly, will discipline follow the children or be kept within the household?

What does this last question mean? Let's say that it is Friday afternoon and your 7-year-old calls to you, "Mommy, come and see." When you get to his room you find the most beautiful rainbow you have ever seen... drawn in permanent magic marker across the door. Since he has made forays into inappropriate art in the past you say, "That's it! I have had it. You are grounded for the weekend. No TV, no computer, and no-phone." Just then you hear "toot-toot, beep-beep," and its your (soon-to-be) ex coming to pick up the child for their weekend together.

The question is, does the discipline (in the above example, grounding) follow the child to the other parent's home, or wait until the child returns? There is no absolute "right" answer, however it would be a good idea for the two of you to have an understanding in advance of how these situations will be handled. (You don't have a 7-year-old? Substitute a 14-year-old punching a hole in the wall, or a 16-year-old coming in two hours late from a date.)

Genna and Simon believed that discipline should remain in the home and be administered by the parent who dispensed it. They established "house rules," posted them in each home, and agreed that each would administer the discipline in their own homes, unless it was a "major" infraction, which would be handled by both.

Galen and Lucas discussed and agreed that they had never seen eye-to-eye when it came to child rearing. They knew they would set up different rules for each household. They were able to agree that it would be good for the children to see the rules in writing (to make the rules more concrete), and that they would share copies of the "house rules" with each other so that the children would know what was expected in each household.

Evan and Caitlin had five children and found it hard to keep track of all of them at the same time. They decided to establish house rules for each child that would be the same in each household. They printed these rules on paper and posted them in each home, along with the discipline that would be used if the children did not follow the rules. They also agreed to continue family meetings — consisting of Mom, Dad, and all five children — so that these rules and other information could be regularly discussed and negotiated.

Decisions, Decisions, Decisions

It is not unusual for each parent to feel that he or she has had a greater impact on the child's upbringing and has "done more" than the other parent. Obviously, both parents cannot have "done more." In many families, one parent will feel that the other parent was "uninvolved with the children in the past," and "is not likely to be involved in the future." There are several possibilities to consider if this is your feeling.

It is possible — in fact even likely — for a parent faced with the possible loss of contact with children to change previous behavior and even adjust his or her values. It is a common human characteristic to take people and things for granted when they are constant and close at hand, and to try to hold on to them when there is a chance of loss.

It is possible that the other parent tried to have more interaction and involvement, and felt overpowered or unheard with regard to the parenting of the children. Some parents who don't like conflict will keep a low profile about issues — even when they feel strongly about something — just to avoid an argument.

It is possible that the other parent was not as involved in the past as they could or should have been. Does this mean they should not be allowed to be involved in the future? If the children needed this other parent in the past, wouldn't it be valuable for them to have contact now?

As with all other communications, positive problem-solving and decision-making discussions are useful. Negative, punitive, and threatening communications will only get in the way of a cooperative effort to resolve issues together. It is important for you to talk about how the major decisions will be made. Do both parents want input into the decision making? Do they want to divide responsibility for decision making such that each parent will handle decisions in a particular area? (For example, one parent might be responsible for religious and educational decisions while the other parent might be responsible for decisions regarding medical treatment and social activities.) Shall each parent be responsible for the decisions involving one or more children?

It is also possible for you and your partner to arrive at certain commitments now that will decide the future in any of the major areas. For example, you may mutually agree on how the children will be brought up from a religious standpoint. If you can agree, there may not be a need to continue to negotiate in this area.

> **Debbie and Russ** discussed long and hard how to handle decision making. The children had been raised as Catholics. While Russ was not very active in the church, he agreed that they should continue practicing the same religion in the future. He also wanted to have input, as did Debbie, in the other major child rearing areas. The couple agreed to stipulate on the religious upbringing of the children, and to share the decision making jointly regarding education, health care, behavioral standards, and social activities.

In situations where one parent proposes to have responsibility for making all decisions about all the children, several things need to be kept in mind: First, this may be appropriate for some couples in some situations. There may be the feeling that this was the pattern established prior to the separation or divorce and there is no reason why it can't be continued. This feeling is very seldom 100% realistic. Even though one parent may have, apparently, made the decisions, both parents were ultimately responsible for the result or any effects that those decisions and activities may have had.

Second, it may seem a wise choice for one parent to have the decision-making responsibility in order to avoid further conflict and communication. This may appear especially true in situations where the couples feel they cannot talk to each other or deal with each other. *Experience has shown, however, that couples can learn how to communicate about the children and co-parent effectively together, even though they can no longer live together.* Of course, this is only true when both parents can focus on the children, and agree to invest energy toward a cooperative effort.

Third, it should be remembered that the responsibility for child rearing is a monumental task which places parents under considerable stress in the best of situations. This task becomes even more stressful when there is no one to fall back on, or to share concerns and considerations with. In the emotional time of separation and divorce, having one parent responsible for all decision making may be an unfair and unnecessary additional burden.

Fourth, each of you must examine, very closely, whether you are asking for the sole custodial responsibility because of the best interests of the children, or as a function of your own emotional situation. In the latter case, it's likely that:

• you feel the breakup of the marital situation was extremely painful with the loss of the partner and that you could "not bear to lose" the children as well.

• that you feel you must "fight" for the children to protect them and "prove" your love for them.

• you don't really want the children full time, but feel you must fight for them because "good parents fight for their kids."

• you want to "punish" your partner by withholding (controlling) the children, and thereby the other parent.

While these feelings are quite common and understandable, they are not very helpful in terms of co-parenting and child rearing. For example, *research has shown that in families where there is expected to be a transfer of money for either spousal or child support, payment was most consistent and continuous where the paying partner had frequent contact with the children and reasonable input into their upbringing.*

What may be useful is for you is to attempt a "trial run" that you and your partner work out, defining how the decisions will be made for a specified period. You can then carry on this "trial" with the knowledge that if either of you is unhappy with the way things are working, you can renegotiate alternative approaches. You may want to spell out two or three alternatives, either trying them all, or moving from one to another only if the current one is not working. Keep in mind that changes must be by mutual agreement of both parents. At the end of the trial period you may need to get together again and renegotiate.

Tie-breaker

If the two of you decide on joint decision-making ("joint custody"), it may be wise for you to also explore how you will handle potential situations on which you cannot agree. When joint custody is selected, it is wise to have a tie-breaker or safety net built in to the parenting plan. Take, for example, a situation in which your child had difficulty in school (possibly because of the stress and pressure of the separation). At the end of the school year you and your partner are called in by the teacher and guidance counselor and told that your child's grades are marginal. The child has not failed all subjects — if he had, they would have to hold him back — nor has he succeeded in passing enough subjects to be automatically moved ahead. Rather, the school counselor points out that you have a choice: you can either hold the child back and repeat the school year, working toward better skills, or you can pass the child along to the next grade to keep up with friends and attempt to help him catch up through tutoring and other support services. The school staff says that this is the parent's joint decision.

Now imagine that you and your partner each have a different viewpoint. One wants to hold the child back, and the other feels that it is important for the child to stay with his peer group. The question here it is not what you would do in such a situation, rather, how would you break such a tie? The options include:

• Mutually selecting a relative or close family friend who would agree to act as a tie breaker. (Someone who would be comfortable in making a decision they felt was in the best interests of the child.)

• Use mediation.

• Agree to use a neutral and professional third party who has skills and knowledge in the area of disagreement. (An educational expert who would listen to the viewpoint of both parents — and possibly the student and school — and then make a decision.)

• Allow each parent to retain the final decision-making responsibility in specific areas. (One parent could have final say in health and education areas, where the other has final say in religion and behavior standards.)

As you can see, there is no single right answer here, any more than in any of the other issues we have addressed. Rather, it is up to the two of you to establish, beforehand, how you will handle this area.

Custody

You will have noticed by now in our discussion of co-parenting that we have not yet dealt with the issue of custody. Many people don't understand legal custody, and confuse it with where the children will live (sometimes called "physical" or "residential custody").

Legal custody is generally understood to mean which parent has responsibility for decision making in such major areas as education, religion, and health. "Custody battles" in court often deal with many issues beyond, such as contact schedules, holidays, and vacations. The amount of time that children spend with either parent does not necessarily dictate who will make the major child-rearing decisions. The only thing that remains constant about "custody" as a legal term is parental decision making, not child residence. Thus, the issue of "custody" revolves around the responsibility for decision making in major areas of child rearing: religious upbringing, educational upbringing, medical treatment, behavior standards, and social activity. It is my recommendation that, where possible, the parents should work out all other issues of parenting before dealing with decision making. This will make it easier for parents to discuss and agree on decision making later.

Joint Custody. Let's look at the major types of custodial relationships. Since joint custody is the most misunderstood, we will start there. In joint custody, both parents have co-decision-making power with regard to the child-rearing issues: religion, education, behavior standards, medical treatment, and social activity. The children's residential patterns are not directly related to decision-making responsibility. The children may spend more time with one parent than with the other as the daily schedule determines. Attempts to split their time equally between the parents is a misunderstanding of the intent of joint custody. (This is not to say that such schedules can't work out for some families. While some couples strive for an exact 50-50 split on a weekly, monthly or yearly basis, other families find that other proportions or specific schedules better meet the needs of the children and the parents.) It is the co-parenting interaction — the joint decision-making on major issues — that is important in "joint custody," not what color socks the children should wear when they go to school. Thus, a "joint custodial" situation is one in which both parents have input into the major decisions made regarding child rearing. The amount of time the children spend with each parent is a separate decision that does not directly relate to a joint custodial relationship.

> **Hilda and Sam** were clear that neither wanted total decision-making responsibility. They had acted as a team in child rearing in the past, and the team had performed rather well. They wanted to continue a team effort, and therefore agreed to a "joint custodial" relationship in terms of decision making, even though the children were spending most of their time with Sam.

Sole-custody. In sole custody, one parent is responsible for the major decision making regarding child rearing. These decisions are made by the custodial parent. Where there is a sole custodial parent, there is a non-custodial parent. That parent has the right to expect that the parenting arrangement will continue on a consistent basis, regardless of the decision making. Visitation is both a right and a responsibility of parenthood: the non-custodial parent has the right to expect regular contact with the children; the custodial parent and the children have the right to expect that the schedule agreed upon by both parents will be followed on a consistent and dependable basis, not just when convenient.

> **Ken and Joanne** didn't need to discuss much at all, since they had already reached an understanding that Joanne would have sole custody of the children. Ken was very supportive of this idea. Exploration determined that this was not a fight, battle, or a power struggle between the parents. Rather, it was a rational judgment that Joanne was in the best position to make the major decisions and to take that responsibility. She did acknowledge, however, that she would appreciate input from Ken concerning child rearing.

Split Custody. Split custody is a situation that can only occur when there is more than one child. In split custody each parent takes responsibility for decision making for specific children. Again, where the children reside is not the major issue, rather it is who will make the major decisions regarding child rearing practices. Typically, in split custody situations, custodial parents do have greater contact with the child for whom they have responsibility. Exceptions to this occur when the children may be away at school or in some other situation outside of the family unit. In split custody, each parent has custody of one or some of the children, and rights and responsibilities of visitation with the children not in their custody.

> **Jay and Rhonda's** children were 14 and 12, and they agreed their son would stay with Jay, and their daughter would spend her time primarily with Rhonda. It made sense to the parents to have a split custodial relationship in which Jay was responsible for decision making regarding their son, and Rhonda with regard to their daughter.

Other Considerations

You and your partner may wish to discuss any other concerns you have revolving around co-parenting. Care should be taken to make statements in a positive, constructive way. In most cases it is useless and unwise to try to make restrictions or agreements which control the other partner's behavior. A negative example would be to agree that the children can't be with you on the nights you play volleyball. These types of restrictions only attempt to control the other partner, without really adding anything positive to the child-rearing practices. The basic assumption in co-parenting is that neither parent would knowingly or purposely put the children at risk or in danger. There is an expectation that each parent will provide loving, nurturing, rational care for the children in a manner consistent with the best interests of the children.

Under certain circumstances, of course, the children may be at risk. If you seriously believe that this is the case (usually when there is a history of abuse), then you may want to qualify the child contact with the (alleged) abusive parent in a positive way: that the children will have contact with the abusive parent only in the presence of another individual acceptable to both partners, and that the abusive parent is to seek treatment and be willing to verify that the treatment is ongoing. *Remember, just because someone wants a separation or divorce, doesn't want to live with you anymore, and/or is going out with other people, doesn't mean that person is crazy, or untrustworthy and will harm the children.* It may simply mean that he or she has changed and wants a new life or lifestyle. Do not automatically assume that the children are at risk.

If you have reason to seriously suspect abuse, take appropriate steps to investigate thoroughly. Abuse of children (physical, sexual, or emotional) is a crime in most states. If you are aware of child abuse having taken place, you should report it to the appropriate authorities (usually the Department of Social Services).

If you use untrue threats or claims of child or spousal abuse against the other parent as a bargaining chip for dealing with co-parenting or any other issue, you are making the children pawns in a game in which there will be no winners.

What's Left?
There are two other issues that I want to discuss before leaving this already-long chapter. The first has to do with involving the children in the negotiations, and the second has to do with adult children living at home.

Children's' Involvement. There are many parents who want to involve the children in the negotiation process or, at the very least, ask the children, "Which parent do you want to stay with?" A word of caution: Most professionals agree that taking the children's ideas and views into account is a fine idea; directly *asking the children who they want to stay with is probably not a good idea.* That question can put too much pressure on younger children, and older children may not give you a reliable answer.

There is an old story about the parents who asked their child, "If Mom and Dad were both in a row boat in the middle of the ocean and we both fell in, which one of us would you jump in and save?" The implication is that if the child saves Mom, Dad will drown, and if he saves Dad, Mom will drown. This is terrible to ask children to make such a weighty decision. It places them in the position of having a life-or-death responsibility. While not a life-or-death decision, the responsibility is just as weighty when asking the child, "Which parent do want to live with?" The child has to decide, "Who needs more help? Who needs me more?" With teens, you also have to be concerned that their answer may be based on more self-serving principles. For example, where does their current boyfriend or girlfriend live? Who will let them stay up later? Who will let them have the car more often? While important issues to teens, they are not necessarily a good basis on which to make a decision. Rather, if children are to be involved in setting up a parenting plan, it makes more sense for the parents to decide how they would like the plan to work, and then to ask the children, "How can we improve this plan?" In this way, the parents are still seen as being in charge, and the children get to have input for improving the plan but not responsibility for development of the plan (and perhaps using faulty logic to do so).

Older Children. Here is an area of concern that, while not a legal issue, is still an important parenting dilemma. How you handle adult (over 18) children who still live at home? While many children want to get out of the home as soon as possible, there are some who can't get out, or who return after finding out about the real world, seeking shelter and reassurance. Whatever the reason, whatever the age, parents will want to discuss questions that include:

- Where will the adult child stay?
- What are her responsibilities?
- Will he pay rent?
- Can she come and go as she pleases?
- How long can he stay?
- How — if that all — will we support her?

These questions apply both to children who are in college and those who are not. Some parents also feel these questions apply to children living outside the home, as well. As with everything else, there are no right or wrong answers. It may, however, be important for you to discuss these issues if you have, or are likely to have, such a situation arise in the near future. If you do not discuss these issues and share in the support, one of you is likely to feel overburdened with the responsibility.

There is a great deal of material to digest in this chapter. If you or your partner have trouble with any of the issues discussed here, please contact a mediator or a licensed family therapist for help.

"Homework" for the Division of Property Discussion

Both partners should complete each assignment in *writing prior to the discussion of this topic*. Bring the written work to the session. When "several" items are suggested, prepare two or more

Reading — Read chapter 5, "Division of Property," before completing the following assignments. Read and follow the agenda for this topic provided in Appendix A.

Household property — Both partners should prepare a master inventory list of all household items. Prepare individual lists of those items you would like to keep.

Assets and liabilities — Both partners should prepare a list of all major assets and debts. Each should then prepare several lists of possible property divisions that would be acceptable to you. Make sure to include both assets and debts.

5

Division of Property
Whose Teapot Is That, Anyway?

WHEN PEOPLE TALK ABOUT THE DIVISION OF PROPERTY as a result of separation or divorce, they are generally talking about *marital property*. When the courts talk about the division of property as a result of separation or divorce, they are only talking about marital property. The difference is that you may jointly elect to divide marital, non-marital, both, or neither. Since you are not bound by a court's decision — unless you end up in court — you have the flexibility to do what seems right for your family. Some couples decide to follow the guidelines established by state law or court rule, while others negotiate outcomes that would never be "ordered" in a court of law, but which will be honored and enforced by the same court, when jointly agreed-upon and incorporated into a separation agreement.

Marital Property
Generally speaking, marital property consists of all property obtained since the date of the marriage and prior to a signed document of separation. Domestic laws differ from state to state with regard to the definition of marital property. Some states use the philosophy of "community property"; other states use "equitable distribution" or "title. " While it is good to know the state statute under which you and your spouse are negotiating, it is not necessarily essential to use these definitions in your negotiation. In most jurisdictions, you and your spouse can define marital property any way that seems fair to both of you — as long as you both agree. State statutes will only come into play if you and your spouse cannot agree and therefore end up in court.

Non-marital Property
Not everything is considered marital property. Non-marital property includes inherited property passed on to one of the

spouses (real estate or any other valuable asset), gifts to either spouse (as opposed to gifts to the couple), and property obtained in exchange for either of these types of items. Assets owned by either spouse prior to the marriage and held aside from the marriage, or directly traceable to pre-marital property, are also generally considered non-marital property. Personal property such as clothes and jewelry given to each other are generally not considered marital property, although there are some exceptions to this, such as when items were obviously bought for investment purposes, or when a family heirloom — such as a wedding or engagement ring — is passed along. Some couples have more difficulty than others in defining whether property is marital or non-marital. If there is a serious question, outside help should be sought. Keep in mind that the strict legal definition may not be helpful (unless you end up in court). Rather, look at what the intent was at the time of the exchange or acquisition. The issue is what you were trying to accomplish then, not what are you trying to get out of — or more of — now.

Identifying Your Assets and Liabilities

To divide marital property, you'll want to develop a list of all assets and liabilities (more homework), first individually, and then jointly. Focus initially on listing the items, not their value. For convenience sake, the items might be grouped into several categories such as the ones listed below. (An outline to help refresh your memory, and a more complete list appear in Appendix D.)

Real estate: family residence... business property... vacation property... investment property. *Other property:* stocks, bonds, other securities... savings and bank accounts... vehicles — automobiles, boats, R.V.'s and motorcycles... contract options... life insurance... pensions and other retirement funds (IRAs, CDs, TSPs, 401(k)'s... business and professional practices and assets.

Debts and Liabilities: Loans... charge accounts... mortgages... outstanding bills

A note and word of caution: In listing assets and liabilities, "all" assets and liabilities (both marital and non-marital) should be listed. While only marital property is generally divided between the couple, it is important for each of you to know what non-marital property exists as well. Non-marital assets and liabilities may affect the division of marital property (and later the ability to provide spousal or child support).

Value

After you have listed all property items and debts, begin to assign each item a value. It may be necessary to get some of the items appraised by experts in order to assign a value as accurately as possible. Misjudging the value of your home by several thousand dollars — a distinct possibility in a volatile real estate market — may cause an imbalance in the final division of marital property. Incidentally, "expert" appraisal does not mean Uncle Joe or Aunt Sally who have "some knowledge. " Rather, you should approach a neutral party with no vested interest or connection to either of you. You can, of course, obtain a second or third appraisal if you are not satisfied with the initial assessment. If several assessments are obtained, you may wish to average all appraisals in order to arrive at a fair and equitable value. You need not establish value down to the penny; however, it is important that you satisfy yourself that you have fully investigated all items with an uncertain value. Whether the house is worth $182,500 or $183,000 is not important; whether the house is worth $180,000, $190,000, or $200,000 is. In establishing a value, a "paid" appraisal is not always necessary, but can be used if you prefer. Many real estate agents provide a comprehensive evaluation with "comps" (comparable sales) as a free service. Make sure you use someone who has experience and has no prior contact with either of you. If the separation has not yet occurred, you may not want to tell the agent about the separation. In this way you can avoid the "fire sale" attitude that is sometimes built into the calculation when the agent thinks the separation will force a fast sale and lower price.

Susan and Martin didn't have very much. They came from poor families and started off their marriage with very little income and no assets. When they decided to separate, their bank accounts were minimal, their mortgage was maximal, and their future vision somewhat fanciful. However, they didn't have much in the way of non-mortgage debt. They had kept their charge accounts paid in full each month; they were not over-extended, and they even had some equity in the house since they had been living there about eight years. A little investigation showed that if the house were sold, after expenses they could each net approximately $20,000 dollars. Initially, they decided to put the house on the market, splitting the net proceeds when it sold. They also worked out arrangements as to how the mortgage and other expenses would be paid while they were waiting for the house to sell. Then they began to consider what other options existed besides selling the house. They learned that Susan, who made slightly more than Martin, could probably obtain a second mortgage on the house for about $20,000 since her credit record was clean, her salary was reasonably good, and she had no outstanding debts. Susan was willing to take in a roommate who would pay $450 a month and share the utilities. The couple agreed that Susan could keep the house and buy out Martin's share, giving Martin the money he needed to make a down payment on the two-bedroom condo he was interested in.

Business Property

As you will have noticed in the outline above, one potential marital asset is an independently-owned business or professional practice. While discussion of marital property is difficult as a whole, it is often even more difficult for couples to discuss division of businesses or professional practices. Valuation of such property may require the use of a professional expert skilled in evaluating or appraising businesses in that field. Even when professional experts are used, there is not always a clear-cut answer to the value of the business. This is especially true in any service business (as opposed to manufacturing where there is equipment, stock and future contracts to fill). The couple may wish to use multiple experts, obtain several opinions, and average these together. It then remains to negotiate how division or economic balancing can take place in order to complete the overall division of marital property equitably. This is a complex area — go slowly, but don't drag your feet. Take your time, so that each spouse understands what the numbers are and what they mean. If, in the past, you have heard your spouse say the business is "worth a half a million," or "grosses $500,000," it doesn't mean that you are necessarily entitled to $250,000. Even if it does, you may also be responsible for a proportion of the overhead and expenses. Depending on one's needs and the field of business activity, it is possible to assign different values to the same business beyond the absolute value of the stock, inventory, equipment, and materials on hand. Additionally, many private practices and service oriented businesses rely to a large extent on the name of the person who is operating the business entity.

Janet and Dan owned a small restaurant and both worked there at various times. Dan was the general manager; Janet took care of the books, the payroll, and served as hostess on many occasions. One reason people came to the restaurant was the way Janet and Dan related to the customers. They chose not to continue working together and opted for a buyout. To evaluate the business, each of them made their own fair market value estimates, obtained a professional appraisal and, finally, averaged the three figures. They were careful not to negotiate who would buy out the other until after the value had been calculated, so their individual estimates would not be unfairly biased. After the value was determined, they decided who would purchase the restaurant, and then worked out the terms.

One of the reasons couples often have difficulty discussing this particular area is that the spouse who owns (operates) the professional practice or business is afraid that the other spouse will want to interfere and control how the business is run, or put a drain on the business long after the marriage is over. While this may not be a legal reality, it is still often a concern. Tread carefully but firmly in this area. Reassure, or ask for reassurance, about the intent and philosophy with regard to handling the business. Do not threaten or cajole. Investigate all options and alternatives, list them on a separate sheet of paper as you go along, and discuss each one prior to making a joint decision. Remember also not to "kill the goose that laid the golden egg. " If you demand your share of the business (or practice), and the business goes into extreme debt and fails, you may be left with nothing (or even worse). Explore ways that you can both benefit. Sometimes this means trading off business value against some other assets. Sometimes it means the payoff will need to take place over time, so as not to place undue burden on the cash flow. If you want a lump sum, consider cosigning the note so that if the business goes south, you each have a responsibility for the debt as well as the profit. If you are unwilling to consider these kinds of options, are you really working toward a win-win outcome? "Not killing the goose" also means realizing that your family may have benefited from "write-offs" and other expenses (insurance, cars, gas, phone, computer) absorbed by the business. If the business is destroyed or diminished it may mean greater expense and belt tightening for everyone in the family. Just because she spent all her time at work and not at home (your view) doesn't mean there was no benefit to the family.

Household Property
In general, one of the easiest ways to divide household property (pots, pans, furniture, electrical appliances, and all the "stuff" you have accumulated over the years) is simply for each spouse to walk into every room in the house with a pad and pencil and write down all items contained in the room. Care must be taken not to overlook items. A useful technique is to walk in the doorway, turn right, sweep the room slowly with your eyes, and write down everything you see. Where there are drawers, cupboards, cabinets,

shelves, desks, closets, and dressers, contents should be investigated and the items catalogued. Do this carefully – there is always a tendency to "not see" the stuff you have been looking at for years. This list should be made between sessions as part of your homework. After all items have been recorded separately, compare your lists for oversight and make a master list of all items by combining your list with that of your partner. Now take the master list and make a separate list of those items each would like to have. Then, at an appointed time, sit down together with your individual "want" sheets and the master list. Check off each item on your respective lists that is not on the list of your partner. If it's on your list and not on their list, you get it. Similarly, if it's on their list and not on your list, they get it. Now, look at what is left. Items on both lists — or neither list —should be reviewed and discussion should commence with regard to negotiating who gets what. For example, your list might reflect the following items:

couch	*stereo*
coffee table	*TV*
bookcase	*video recorder*
living room picture	*microwave*

Your ex's list could include:

dining room table & chairs	*stereo*
dining room lamp	*TV*
dining room mirror	*video recorder*
piano	*microwave*

Those items which are unique to each list — couch, coffee table, bookcase and living room picture for you; dining room furniture, mirror, and piano for your spouse — will be put on your individual lists. The items that are listed in common — stereo, TV, video tape recorder, and microwave — will need to be discussed to determine how the division will take place. Rationale for division can be based on need, use, or value.

Value of Household Items
The value of household items is the least productive means of division (unless we are talking about very valuable items). Household items are very difficult to value. Most people start off

wanting to negotiate value based on the cost when new. They fail to realize that most of the household items are not new; in fact, they may be well worn and not worth much money. Divisions that are based on need, sentimental value, or feel are generally more satisfactory. If you divide based on value, make sure that each of you are using the same frame of reference. There are several levels of valuation that can be used, including the price when purchased, current fair market value, replacement value (new or used), or the value of the item if sold (at a yard sale or in the paper). Unless it belonged to Paul Revere, that silver service you got as a present isn't nearly as valuable as you might think. When the list is very long and "horse trading" is difficult, you may prefer to use another technique: place all of the items mutually desired on a combined list, flip a coin to see who starts, then alternate back and forth, choosing one item at a time off the list. Scratch chosen items from the combined list and place them on each person's list as you go along. A flip of a coin might let the other person start and, using the list from above, she might choose the stereo; then you might then choose the microwave from the three remaining items. She then has her choice of the two remaining items, with the last item going to you.

Again, let me stress that experience has shown that the functional use or need of items — rather than value — is a more practical manner for negotiating division than is dollar value. A couple may choose not to split up a dining room set (because two halves of the dining room set will satisfy neither party), and choose instead to trade off a bedroom set or other furnishings or possessions. Where both need the same item, another alternative is to buy a dining room set of equal value out of joint marital assets so that each partner can have roughly equivalent possessions. Where several items are to be purchased, each can end up with some old and new "stuff. "

John and Erin worked out a deal that was satisfactory to both, but by no means equal in terms of value. It was, however, quite fair, since both ended up with things that they wanted. When all of the pots, pans, cooking utensils, sheets and pillowcases, books, furnishings, and appliances had been divided, there was one thing left on their list: a recliner that had both heat and vibration elements. John used it after his "old man's" football practice, and Erin used it after aerobics. They had both grown attached to the chair and both wanted it. Everything else was divided down the middle, and the division was as about as equal as could possibly be. While they could have flipped a coin for the chair, that solution would not suit them. Instead, they started offering each other, in trade for the recliner, items which they had previously divided. Ultimately, Erin offered John the clothes washer for the recliner. John accepted, and the couple proceeded with the division of other assets and liabilities.

Monica and Paul agreed that each was entitled to half of the marital assets. However, the different situations in which they would be living after the separation made equal division of the household property impractical. They first made a complete list of items to be divided, then took a look at their respective needs. Since Paul was moving into a smaller apartment, the larger pieces of furniture and oversized chairs would not look good nor suit his needs. He and Monica divided the pots and pans, silverware, dishes, books, and other items, then agreed that Paul would use some of the joint savings account to purchase some smaller but more appropriate furnishings for his apartment. They agreed that some of Paul's personal possessions could be stored in the attic of the house. (Monica was to stay in the residence for a maximum of three years) If Paul wanted any of his items, he had to notify Monica one week in advance to come over and pick them up.

Although the above guidelines for division of household furnishings generally apply, the couple should be sensitive to the fact that there may be a few items that have sentimental value to either or both spouses. Functional or useful need may be minimal, indeed the value of such items may be minimal, but they may have some other meaning for you. For example, if Aunt Jane passed down the hand-carved wooden bowl, it may at first view be considered marital property since it was a wedding gift, and indeed may have been used throughout the marriage. However, since the bowl has been on that side of the family for three generations, you might try to acknowledge the sentimental attachment (whether familial or not) and adapt your list accordingly.

> **Bradley's mother** had given his wife, Jessica, a family heirloom – a silver tea service that actually had been passed down from the time of Paul Revere. The tea service was old and very valuable, and often brought out as a serving piece on holidays and other festive occasions. Both spouses had vested interest in the tea service because it represented something special (beyond its intrinsic value). After discussing various options and acknowledging that each had a reasonable interest, they agreed to share the tea service, both having access to it during the year by alternating where it would stay and who got to use it for the various holidays. Jessica and Bradley agreed that the tea service would be passed on to the first of their children to be married.

Once all of the items have been divided, make a master list showing which person gets which items. Make several copies, so each of you can have a copy and one can be appended to the separation agreement at the appropriate time, if necessary. (Many couples choose not to append such lists of assets since separation agreements ultimately become a matter of public record. Rather, they simply refer to existing lists in separation agreements). You may also want to mark each item (red and blue sticker dots work well) to make division easier. Put the dots on the bottom of the items so that identification is easier and quicker when the physical division is to take place.

Title

Keep in mind that the way a property is held in title (legal ownership) during the marriage, does not necessarily define who will end up with that property. Nevertheless, the list of major assets and liabilities should include how the property is titled, not so much for how it will end up, but as a reminder of what titles and ownership papers may have to be changed when the division is effected.

Pensions

When dealing with division of retirement accounts, you'll need to be careful and possibly do some homework (or at the very least gather some specific information). Some retirement funds are difficult to divide immediately because some pension companies will not allow access to these funds nor allow loans against them. In the past, some would not even write two separate checks at retirement time; this has changed. Many pensions cannot be liquidated before retirement, and although some can, there is often a penalty for early withdrawal. This needs to be investigated quite carefully. An accountant, tax specialist or someone in the pension department, can be very helpful in gathering necessary information.

Retirement accounts are also difficult for some couples to deal with because they have emotional as well as financial implications. They represent a person's or family's future security. Many people feel threatened when discussing their pension (retirement) account. This is quite natural. If you or your partner own a pension or retirement account, it is not unusual to "feel" that your future is threatened if you have to share or divide the pension. For some reason it is easier for many people to divide a savings account than it is a pension, even though they are similar in nature. The same people who will divide a savings account without blinking an eye will sometimes have difficulty even discussing pensions. This is not always the case but does happen with some regularity. Pensions (and other retirement accounts) are really nothing more than an enforced savings plans. As such, they are the same as a savings or investment account, except (and this is done purposely) you can't get into them whenever you want to.

If you look at pension/retirement accounts as savings accounts for the future, you may find them be easier to deal with. One of the issues in pension-sharing discussion is the length of time a person is in a pension. The issue here is the time in the pension before, during, and after the marriage. Here are some important questions to consider:

• If a person is in a pension for 20 years, and married for the last 10 years, what portion of the pension should each partner get?

• What if the person works for 10 years after the marriage? Is the other spouse entitled to any portion of the money earned (and set aside) from non-marital (after-the-marriage) energies?

• What does "after the marriage" mean? Does it mean after a separation agreement or after divorce?

If you decide to divide a pension you will most likely need a "QDRO" — Qualified Domestic Relations Order (usually pronounced "quad-ro") — which is a separate document, approved by the court at divorce, that authorizes the company managing the pension to divide the pension into two separate, predefined accounts, one for each spouse.

Like almost all the other issues discussed in this book, there are no right or wrong answers. It is important, however, to discuss and negotiate an outcome that is acceptable to both of you.

Valuing Pensions

Pensions are one of those areas that can be quite tricky and you may need expert help. Pensions come in different flavors and are often not easy to value. This is an asset that needs to be looked at carefully.

Most pensions provide a year-end summary sheet which is sent to the owner each December or January. These statements give an estimate of the value but the amount shown is not necessarily accurate, since they may only reflect what has been contributed by the individual and not by the company. Often, the summary sheet will identify a monthly payment figure rather than the total value of the account. These annual statements usually show the amount that you will receive at retirement if you do not work any longer for that company and the money stays in the pension account until retirement age.

Your first step is to contact your pension plan administrator and ask for a calculation of the value of your pension. Some will

Dick and Joanne had been married for 30 years. During that time, Dick had two jobs. He retired from his first job with the military after 20 years, and began drawing a small retirement. After a year off he found a new job. Dick plans on working at least five more years in his new position, and understands that he will not be "vested" in his current pension for at least one more year. He also understands that the company he works for may be bought out, and as a result of downsizing, his job may be in jeopardy. Dick and Joanne discussed these issues and agreed that for the past thirty years they had planned on living off of his retirement account when he retired. They recognized that his current pension plan was in jeopardy if he did not become vested before he left. They also recognized that if he did work five more years, the pension should have some moderate value. Finally, the couple discussed the fact that Joanne also had returned to the workforce and had a small pension of her own. Based on the discussions above, they agreed to split all three pensions using a "QDRO" for each and agreed that the division would be calculated based on Dick working five more years, because that had been their plan all along. They agreed that if Dick worked less time, they would divide those accounts. They also agreed that if Dick decided to work longer, Joanne would not be entitled to any of the income from his additional efforts. That is, she was entitled to fifty percent of his military pension and fifty percent of his civilian pension up to 14 years. Any pension value that Dick obtained beyond fourteen years was credited to him. Additionally, Dick would be entitled to one-half of Joanne's pension until the same date (the fourteen-year mark). Like Dick, any additional pension value that Joanne accrued by working longer would be credited to her alone.

provide this information without much fuss; others are a bit resistant because it means more work and because they are reluctant to estimate certain information necessary in calculating.

Another approach to valuation is to contact someone who sells annuities and ask the cost of an annuity that would pay the monthly amount that the pension is projecting. You'll need to tell the person you talk to how many years the money will sit and gain interest before payout (time until you retire), since this is an important part of the calculation.

The third method is to contact a CPA or accountant or one of the firms that specializes in pension valuations. There is generally a charge for this service but the information should be pretty accurate.

Finally, if you are planning to share one or both pensions at retirement, you can simply devise a formula for division, and let the pension department calculate the outcome when the pensions are paid out. You can of course develop any formula that makes sense to both of you.

Lisa and Joe were married for thirty-three years. During that time, Lisa's primary work had been as a homemaker. Not until the last five or six years had she begun to work outside the home and her income was still quite small. They had lived in their current house for over twenty years and had developed close to $100,000 in equity. With five years to go on their mortgage, they had monthly payments of only $197. Because of the length of the marriage and the large discrepancy between their incomes, they agreed to trade Joe's share of the house against Lisa's share of the pension. That is, Lisa basically "bought Joe out" of his share of the house, with her share of his pension. They agreed that Joe would continue to make monthly payments until the mortgage was paid off (this would be called "alimony"), then continue the payment of $197 a month directly to her as alimony. The alimony would stop if she remarried. If Lisa sold the house prior to Joe's retirement (four years away at the earliest), she had the option to split the equity with Joe and receive half of his pension when he retired, or keep the entire home equity and receive nothing more.

Ward and Darby were a young couple whose incomes were enough to meet their needs and to put away a little bit of money at the end of each month. When they separated, Darby had about $4000 in a pension plan that she was unable to liquidate or have access to in any way until she retired. An IRA for Darby, purchased with money from an income tax return several years earlier, had grown to approximately $3500 in value. The couple agreed to sell the house and split the profits, but didn't know how to handle the pension and the IRA account since both were in Darby's name. While she could have paid Ward half of the total of the pension and the IRA, that approach would have left her with little money from her share of the proceeds from the sale of the house. Instead, they transferred ownership of the IRA to Ward. Since this was viewed as a division of marital property, IRS rules allow for such transaction without having to liquidate the account and suffer the ten percent penalty for early withdrawal. They then agreed to give Ward $500 "off the top" from the net profit of the sale of the house, and to divide the remainder equally. In this way, each was able to obtain half of the pot, have relatively equal cash, and have the beginnings of a retirement account that would develop and grow as they got older.

Liabilities

In considering the division of property, the liability sheet is just as important as the asset sheet. You'll find it helpful to make a list of all liabilities, including mortgages, liens, personal or bank loans, and loans against insurance policies, investment accounts, thrift savings plans, pensions, and medical/dental bills. Don't forget outstanding Visa, MasterCard, department store cards, gasoline cards, and any other types of charge cards. In the case of credit card accounts, not only will the debts need to be paid off, discussion will need to be held concerning who is responsible for payment for each account, who can continue to use which accounts, when the use of joint accounts will stop, and who will end up with each account. There are a number of other issues revolving around credit card accounts that we will address later. Don't forget, the division of debt is as much a marital responsibility as the division of assets.

Anne and Gregory had a house with $30,000 equity, a pension worth approximately $7000, an annuity worth $6500, a couple of small bank accounts, and about $1200 worth of outstanding credit card bills. Each had a relatively new automobile, complete with monthly payments. According to their budget, each was just barely able to make ends meet for themselves and the children. Gregory wanted to live in the house, and felt very strongly about it. Anne, for reasons of her own, proposed to split the $1200 credit card debt equally and to waive her right to Gregory's $7000 pension — if he would buy out her share in both the house and the annuity (a total of $18,000 to $19,000). After negotiation, they settled Gregory's counter proposal to pay $10,000 at the signing of the separation agreement and monthly installment payments of $150 until the rest was paid off (including five percent interest). He arranged a second mortgage to cover the initial payment to Anne and to pay off his car.

When it came to dividing assets, **Trish and Henry** didn't have much to divide. Aside from some household "stuff," their old cars and an old sailboat (Henry referred to it as "a hole in the water that you poor money into") all they had was their house. What they did have a lot of was debt. In addition to their mortgage and the boat loan, they had $35,000 in credit card debt. They had been living well above their means, and were falling farther and farther behind each month. After making a list of assets and debts, and looking at their monthly budgets, they determined that it would be foolhardy to start their new lives so deeply in debt (it costs more to live apart that it does to live together). Neither one could afford the mortgage on the house alone, and even together the cost of a second residence was too much to handle. They agreed to sell both the boat and house, and use the money to pay off their debt. They agreed that if anything remained after the debt was paid off, they would share it equally. Additionally, they agreed to close all the joint credit card accounts except one, and to use it only for emergencies, by joint agreement, until the house and boat were sold.

Principles of Property Division

When the list of marital assets and debts is as complete as possible, you are in a position to discuss "the principles" under which the property (assets and debts) will be divided. It is important to work on the principles first. After that, the rest will fall into place. Questions to discuss include:

• Will the property be divided equally, 60-40, or in some other fashion?

• Are there specific items that definitely will go to one partner or the other?

• Is earning potential to be taken into account?

• What is the situation with regard to non-marital assets?

In a family where one spouse has considerable non-marital assets, how will this be calculated into the recipe? (It might be "fair" for the spouse with few, if any non-marital assets, to take a larger share of the marital "property," but this may not be appropriate in all cases. A non-working spouse, or one who makes less money, is nevertheless entitled to an equitable share of the property.) As noted earlier, domestic law differs among the states with regard to how property division may be accomplished once a dispute reaches court. However, you and your spouse can still divide the property and reassign ownership (title) any way you wish, as long as you are both in agreement as to how the division should be handled. One of the guiding principles should be the needs of the partners and the family as a whole. Keep in mind that you are trying to restructure the family in the most effective, fair, and mutually useful way.

Slicing Up the Pie

Once the principles have been established, it's time to set about actually dividing the property. Each partner will obviously have ideas about where various assets and liabilities should go. ("Let's divide it fifty-fifty" sometimes means "I'll take all the assets, you take all the liabilities!") *Care must be taken at this point to maintain a rational discussion. The loss of material objects can feel very threatening. Discussing even potential loss can invoke fear and insecurity that quickly turns to anger and hostility toward the other.* It is quite easy during these discussions for the anger to get out of hand and harsh comments to be thrown back and forth. Care must be taken to minimize this, and partners need permission to terminate a discussion at any time that they are feeling uncomfortable or upset. As before, attempts should be made to set up a time for another discussion after emotions are brought under control. Keep in mind that your goal is how to divide the property, not to resolve your feelings toward one another. Each of you will want to develop a set of proposals (two or more) with regard to how you see the division taking place. Each of these proposals for division is to be discussed in turn. Any or all of the proposals can be modified. When the division is tentatively accepted by both of you, write down your understanding of the proposed division (assets and liabilities, and responsibilities with regard to the division, i. e., transfer of title at such-and-such a date, payoff, buyouts, or transfer of funds to balance other assets, and responsibility for debt.)

Fifty-Fifty?

Keep in mind that you do not necessarily have to divide all property equally. It may be advantageous, either personally or from a financial standpoint, to divide assets and liabilities other than fifty-fifty. Also, there may be some items (even among those that are clearly marital property) which can be taken out of the marital pot and set aside. This happens most often when certain assets or holdings are held in trust for, or given directly to, children. Examples would be a third car that the teenager is using, or a bank account in the child's name to be set aside for college.

Jointly-Held Property

You and your spouse can also decide to hold some property jointly for a set period of time, or until a specific event occurs. This might occur, for example, with a residence or family business. The property can then be liquidated or transferred, according to your joint decision.

Another example of holding an asset jointly would be an investment to be held until a more appropriate (profitable) time for liquidation. If an asset is to be held jointly, you and your spouse need to decide how the asset will be maintained, and under what conditions it will be liquidated or transferred. If one spouse is going to live in a jointly-held house, for example, discussion should include what happens if repairs are needed, what constitutes a necessary repair, and who pays for what. There could be a fixed dollar amount for repairs, beyond which both split the cost. Or there may be only certain items that will be covered, such as the roof, water heater, plumbing, electric, or major appliances.

Remember, marriage is an equal partnership — in the law anyway — and each spouse is entitled to a share of the marital assets, whether they were a direct income provider or a homemaker. The fact that one spouse worked outside the home, while the other stayed home to work, does not mean all marital assets and debts should go to the spouse who was the primary — or sole — wage earner.

"... And Deeper in Debt"

Keep in mind that the more marital debts you get rid of, the easier it will be to start a new life. You may want to consider some type of division of the debt, perhaps in proportion to the division of the assets, or proportional to income. You may wish to discuss the liquidation (sale) of some assets (bank accounts, CDs, the boat or camper), and use of the money to reduce debt. This would allow each of you to start out on more even footing. (I hope neither of you will start off already owing large amounts of money!)

In certain situations where the debt cannot be eliminated by liquidating marital assets, you will need to discuss who will be responsible for which debts. After those negotiations have taken place, you may need to make special, separate arrangements with the creditors to pay off the outstanding debt at a slower or lower rate. Do not hesitate to call or write the credit department of the institution to whom you owe money to make these arrangements. You can also contact one of the consumer credit counseling groups to help you. (If you do use a consumer credit counseling service, check them out first — they are not all on the up-and-up.) The nonprofit credit counseling organizations are often supported by the credit companies themselves. The credit companies have a vested interest in helping credit card holders in debt pay off the debt and are willing to work with individuals to give them better (lower) interest rates or minimum payments. If you are talking to a fee-for-service credit counseling center, make sure to ask how large the fee will be and how they will verify payment to your accounts from the money you pay them. Creditors to whom you owe money would much rather have you take longer to pay than to stop paying completely. If you explain this as a function of your new marital status, most of them will be understanding and respect you for the responsibility you have taken in contacting them before there is trouble.

You may be able to negotiate reduced rates on your own. If you cannot (or are not comfortable doing so) the credit counseling services may be able to help. In your efforts to balance the debt load, you may find a bit of "creative financing" in order. For instance, a debt consolidation loan — often in the form of a second mortgage — may enable you to make equal or even lower monthly payments over a longer period of time. (It is very risky, however , to burden your home with a loan for "everyday" debts. Be sure you will be able to make the payments for the life of the loan before taking this step!)

If you are thinking about transferring your 21% credit card debt to a 9% card, be careful not only about interest rates, but also about what conditions (such as late payments) may trigger higher interest rates, making it cost more in the long run. With those cautions in mind, however, such a plan can make it possible to carry debts that might otherwise make equitable division of property impossible. The first six to eighteen months are usually the most critical — financially as well as emotionally. This is a time when money is often limited and spread the thinnest. Incomes have to go farther, individuals may not be experienced operating at reduced income levels, and there is less room to manipulate funds. People starting off in tight financial situations who also have large debts to pay may find it difficult to make ends meet. It may be necessary for one or both of you to consider a second job or part-time work — at least on a limited basis — to help resolve the marital debt. Taking in a border (roommate), or providing daycare for young children are ways to generate income and in the case of day-care, allows apparent to stay home with young children.

Don't forget the current expenses you're incurring for the divorce itself. Attorney fees, court costs, custody evaluations, appraisals, and other items may add thousands of dollars to your debt load.

Charlie and Jane didn't have much in the way of assets, so on the face of it there was little to divide. What they didn't see initially was that they had a lot of outstanding debt on their gasoline cards and general credit cards; most were maxed to the limit. They were not very good bookkeepers or organizers, so they hadn't kept track of the bills as they came in. Charlie had tried to start a kite-making business in the basement. The business went under (largely a function of his lack of bookkeeping and organizational skills), but not before Charlie had run up a sizable debt on the credit cards to buy supplies and materials — a total of nearly $18,000. Their assets included the house they had lived in for nearly 10 years (with an equity of $30,000), some small savings and checking accounts, and a pension plan from Jane's work valued at $11,000. They agreed to put the house on the market, and when they went to settlement they would each be issued a check for half of the profit. Jane contended that Charlie was responsible for the $18,000 credit card debt because it had been his business, and his lack of ability had caused the downfall of the company. Charlie argued that it was a family business, and Jane had, in fact, helped with the books (or lack thereof), and if there had been any profit she would certainly have shared equally and gladly in the benefits of the additional income to the family. Furthermore, she had been consulted prior to the business being started about credit card purchases. As the discussion continued, the couple came to agree that the business debt was a marital debt, just as a growing, thriving business would have been a marital asset. They also agreed that they didn't want to use all of the money from the sale of the house for debt resolution, since that would leave them with very little to begin anew. Since Charlie's income was somewhat larger, he agreed to take over the monthly mortgage payments until the house was sold. Upon sale of the house, they planned that $14,000 would be used to pay down the credit card debt, and the remaining $4000 in credit card debt would be divided, with Jane owing $1000, and Charlie owing $3,000 (because of his larger salary). They also agreed to equally divide Jane's pension. This way, after the sale of the house, each could start with a small nest egg in cash, and a small start on a retirement fund.

Sale of the House

If you mutually decide to sell your house there are several issues to consider, including, of course, the fair market value (asking price), and who will sell it for you. Other issues you'll need to discuss that are not often thought about include:

- What happens if the house doesn't sell in thirty, sixty, or ninety days?
- After how long will you adjust the asking price?
- Will you adjust the asking price a second or third time?
- How will you adjust the asking price (by percent reduction or flat dollar amount?)
- What is your bottom line in terms of profit?
- What if someone offers a contract for $10,000, $30,000, or $50,000 less than the asking price?
- What if no one is interested in the house at any price?
- Who will stay in the house while you are trying to sell it?
- Who will be responsible for the mortgage payment while you are trying to sell it?
- If one of you stays in the house, what are the responsibilities with regard to household maintenance, upkeep, and repair?
- If you rent the house, what happens to the income from the rental (if you get more than the mortgage amount)?
- What happens if you don't get enough money from the rental to pay the mortgage? How will the debt be handled for the mortgage? Are property taxes included or do you need to pay those as well?

Issues in Joint Ownership of Property

As mentioned earlier, some couples agree to hold certain property in joint ownership for some period of time. This is sometimes done to allow the children to stay in the house in order to minimize disruption for them. Other times it is due to a financial decision (if the house is paid off, has a low mortgage, or if the sales market is particularly poor). For whatever reason, if you decide to hold property in joint ownership, there are number of issues that need to be addressed. These include:

- How long will it be held in joint ownership?
- Who is responsible for the upkeep?

• Who is responsible for any debts incurred as a result of maintaining joint ownership?

• What will happen after the designated time period has lapsed?

• Will there be a right of first refusal for buyout? Who will have it?

• If the property is a boat, vacation property, or R. V. , who will have use of it, and on what schedule or basis can it be used?

Connie and Peter decided that it would be good for the children to stay in the house at least one more year, since the upcoming school year was to be an important one; the oldest was finishing high school, and the youngest child was completing middle school. They agreed that Connie and the children would stay in the house, and that it would not be put up for sale before graduation so that the kids would not be disrupted or distracted at finals. Connie and Peter agreed that at the end of the one-year period, they would discuss and negotiate the sale. Knowing, however, that people change and that they might not be getting along as well they hoped, they agreed to a general set of rules before proceeding. Those included Connie having a "right of first refusal" to buy out Peter's share. They established a formula for calculating his share that included the averaging of two household valuations (appraisals or real estate estimates). If Connie could not afford to buy out Peter's share, Peter could offer to buy out Connie's share using the same calculation. If neither could afford nor wanted the house, it would be put up for sale. They established ground rules before selecting a salesperson (someone both trusted or someone neither had previous contact with), and agreed to use the same approach of averaging two valuations to establish a fair market asking price. They also agreed that if the house had not sold within three months from when it was put on the market, that they would reduce the asking price by five percent, and again by another five percent three months later if it had still not sold. If they had no solid offers in the first six months, they agreed to obtain another real estate agent. They further agreed that Connie would stay in the house until the house sold, and that they would renegotiate budgets, if necessary, after six months of the house not selling. The couple further agreed to share the cost of any major structural repair to major house systems (electric, plumbing, etc.), and any improvements necessary for the sale. They agreed that if major improvements were found to be necessary (they had some concerns about the roof), they agreed to take a second mortgage to pay for the improvements, knowing it could be paid off at closing of escrow, prior to the division of profits.

Credit Cards (again)

Before we close this chapter, let's take another look at credit cards. "Plastic money" forms a central theme in many of our lives. In today's economy more and more companies extend the upper limits of credit with every new holiday season. There are several considerations you and your partner should discuss with regard to the handling of credit cards and credit card debt. As with other property, the first step is to list all credit cards that each of you own. The list should include the name of the company issuing the credit card, in whose name the card is held, who uses the card, the outstanding balance, and the minimum monthly payment. Several issues will need to be considered at this point. Ascertain if the outstanding debts reflect a *family or marital debt*, or an *individual debt*.

A word of caution here: nothing is ever as easy as it sounds. There may be a difference of opinion between you and your spouse as to whether an expense is a "marital debt" or not. Additionally, like many families, you may not have kept close track of how all of the money was used. This is especially true in situations where cash is borrowed against the credit card, and then used in some unrecorded fashion. In most cases couples are able, through discussion and perhaps some digging into the records (if you don't keep the monthly bills you can request copies from the credit card company), to define which accounts or which parts of accounts represent marital expense. You and your spouse then need to discuss how this marital expense will be resolved.

You also want to discuss who will have the responsibility for the accounts, and whether any future charges can be made against these accounts while you are trying to pay them off. You will need to discuss ownership of the accounts and whose name will be removed from joint accounts. On some accounts this is done relatively easily; on others it is more difficult. Some credit card companies will not take just one spouse's name off the account; they prefer to close out the account and ask each spouse to apply separately. Most companies won't remove a name if there is still a debt owed on the account.

A final note about credit cards: there is still a fair amount of gender and financial bias in our country. It may be difficult for a newly separated woman (especially with a lower level of income) to obtain credit cards on her own. *It may be advantageous for a woman to apply for credit cards in her own name while still married.* In doing so, the entire family's income can be noted on the application, and the chances of approval are thereby increased. She will need to be clear that she will be the one responsible for any debts placed on the card.

Remember to record all of your tentative decisions, including who gets what assets and who is responsible for credit cards and other debts.

If you or your spouse have trouble with any of the issues in this chapter, contact a professional mediator for help.

"Homework" for the Support Discussion

Both partners should complete each assignment in writing prior to the discussion of this topic. Bring the written work to the session. When several items are suggested, prepare two or more.

Reading — Read chapter 6, "Support," before completing the following assignments. Read and follow the agenda for this topic provided in Appendix A.

Budget — Prepare one or more budgets reflecting anticipated needs. (Provide optional budgets that take into account varying arrangements for custody and contact.) Include in your proposals priorities for reducing expenses, should that become necessary. Use the budget forms provided in Appendix C to make this process easier.

Income — List several possible ways you could contribute to increased family income if the budget does not balance.

Support — Think about and write down a range of support (child, spousal, or both) which would be acceptable to you. Consider cost of living adjustments; list options for changed circumstances. What changes in your life or in the life of your spouse do you believe should trigger an adjustment? Should such a change be predetermined, or negotiated at the time?

Duration — How long should child or spousal support continue? Should certain life events such as school milestones, age, marital status, or vocational status automatically lead to a reduction, discontinuance, or renegotiation of support?

6

Support

Budgets and Other Money Matters

WHEN I BEGAN TO EDIT THIS CHAPTER, and read the homework assignments I'd suggested at the beginning, I started to feel overwhelmed with all that had to be done. "If this seems like a lot to *me*," I thought, "imagine what it must feel like to those who are overwhelmed by the prospect or reality of separation!" Please do not become afraid (easy for me to say) or so overwhelmed that you throw up your hands and say "what's the use?" This *can* be done! You'll need to give yourself enough time so that you can do it bit by bit. It is doable. It will not be fun. Read the entire chapter before you worry about forms and outlines, so you can see how the process flows. Why don't you stop for second now and get yourself a cup of coffee or a soda, then come back and read chapter in the more relaxed frame of mind.The two major topics of this chapter are *child support* and *spousal support*. Whether or not financial support is provided to one spouse by the other should be based upon the *needs* of all the family members. "Support" is just what it says — help with living expenses — not a punitive award given because one spouse hurt or rejected the other. Most support is time limited, based upon the estimated time for those receiving the support to gain independence.

Budgets
Budgets are important, to see if support is necessary and to see if survival is possible. Even if there are no children, and you each earn the same amount of money, it may still be difficult to survive on your own. Two people cannot live apart as cheaply as they can together. *Budgets will help you see where the money needs to go, and where it can no longer go.* Budgets can help you prepare both financially and mentally for your new lives and lifestyles.

The best way for most people to determine what support is needed is to develop a budget that spells out the needs of all concerned. The budget should be realistic, based upon past experience and future predictions, taking into consideration that *most families will experience some belt tightening and some reduction in the standard of living* they enjoyed during the marriage. Filling out a complete and detailed budget is a lot of work. It is done because it is very important to help establish current and future needs. *To see where the money is going often makes a difference in a partner's willingness to pay.*

In developing budgets, it's helpful to separate expenses for the children from personal expenses for yourselves. If co-parenting schedules have already been agreed upon, it will be easier to project what the child care costs will be (since parents will know how much time they will be caring for the children.) If child care scheduling has not been decided, you may want to go back to that now. If you do not have a child care schedule in place, you will need to develop several alternative budgets that reflect varying amounts of time spent with the children.

I recommend that each spouse prepare a separate proposed budget. These budgets can then be compared and combined into a third overall family budget. It will probably be necessary to make modifications and adjustments to the individual budgets, primarily as a function of the total family income.

Before looking at a sample budget, let's get a few ground rules and understandings out of the way:

• Each individual should be responsible for independently preparing an initial draft of the budget.

• The budget form provided in Appendix C is only an outline. Families often have other expenses that are not included in the outline provided. The blank spaces will allow you to customize your budget to reflect your family's needs.

• Your budget proposal is not a dream list or a wish list. Budgets have to be based on reality — reasonable and realistic financial and living arrangements. Regardless of the reason for the marital breakup, it is unrealistic to expect your spouse to take on a second, third or fourth job, or to live in a small rented room while you live in luxury. (Remember also that "luxury" is in the eye of the beholder.)

• Most households experience a reduction in the standard of living after a breakup. It is unlikely that you will be able to live as cheaply apart as you did together.

• If one of you has not worked in the past, it may be necessary for you to consider work now or in the future in order to achieve the type of financial security and independence you desire. If you expect that you or your spouse will need additional training or education, now is the time to mention it and cover it in the budget (see chapter 8).

Whatever expenses you predict, your budget must be as accurate as possible. It will require some work on your part to come up with these figures.

Include in your budget the family's outstanding debts and liabilities. These obligations must be paid off on a regular basis. If your debts are minimal, the regular payments can easily be included in the budget. If your debts are greater, other means may have to be considered (see chapter 5).

Although it does require additional work, it is useful for your budget to have two columns: one for the direct personal living expenses that you will incur, and one for the expenses attributable to your children. The more specifically you can document each separate need, and divide the cost between yourself and the children, the easier it will be, later on, to assign values for child support or spousal support, if either is necessary.

Creating your budget on a computer spreadsheet will take a few extra minutes initially, but will save time in the long run. Include four columns after the line items and label them *husband, children, wife, children*. In this way the spreadsheet can be used to set up the individual budgets initially, and to combine both budgets after they are prepared. The value of the spreadsheet is that you can add or change items and the columns will be totaled for you as you make changes. It is also possible to total up the two "children" columns so that you can get an idea of the total projected expense and compare that with the total expenses for the children in the past. *An extra and important benefit of using the spreadsheet is that its structured format helps reduce the emotional discomfort.* It won't make working on the budgets fun, but it will make the process less painful.

When you each have prepared a fairly complete budget proposal, it is time to discuss them. Prepare a "master budget sheet" with the same line items that are on your individual budgets, and the same four columns side by side: *husband, children, wife, children*. Record on the master budget all of the information contained on your two separate budget proposals. (You can use a spread sheet on a computer or do it on paper. If you use paper, use a pencil, since you can expect to make some changes!) In filling out the master budget, care should be taken by each spouse not to make any critical comments regarding the other's figures or projections. After all of the numbers have been filled in, add up each column so that you can see what the total projected expenses will be. Keep in mind that this budget is a monthly expense budget, and should be compared with monthly take-home income.

Next is the tough part. Don't be frightened, don't shout, and try not to get upset. After all four columns have been added, those totals need to be added across to see the grand total expense projection. Following this, compare your family's net (after tax) expendable income with the expense total. Keep in mind that even non-marital income must be considered at this point. For example, if one of the spouses has a trust fund or investment that produces $800 a month in interest or dividend, even though this may not be "marital property," this is money which is considered income to that spouse. It is similar to having a job that earns $200 a week. Subtract the expenses from the income and the result will show how much is left over, or how much "in the hole" you would go each month with this projected budget.

	Husband/Child(ren)	Wife/Child(ren)	Total
income			
expense			
total			+/−

The following diagram is an abbreviated example:

Expenses:

Wife		Children		Husband		Children		Grand Total
_____	+	_____	+	_____	+	_____	=	_____

Income:

Husband's Monthly Take Home _____

Other income + _____

Wife's Monthly Take Home + _____

Other Income + _____

Total = _____

Result:

Total Income − Total Expenses = _____

Adjusting the Budget

Most couples find they must sharpen their pencils at this stage. If you find a negative grand total, as do many couples, that's how much "over budget" you are. You'll need to take steps to adjust the expense items to bring them into line with income; or you'll need to find ways of increasing income to meet your expense needs.

Each of you should first review your own projected expenses and attempt to reduce your own items. (If you've completed the "homework" assignment for this chapter, you already have a suggested list of options for trimming your expenses.) As each item is reduced, erased and changed on the master list, the grand totals are changed as well. If you can work in this way to reduce the budget expenses to meet joint income, that's great. Keep in mind that line items on the budget have to be realistic, and that projecting too low an expense will only lead to frustration in staying within the budget later on.

If, after reducing your own side of the budget, there is still a negative cash projection, I recommend a collaborative effort. Take a careful look at each other's budget, (gently) ask questions about projected expenses, and make (tactful) suggestions about reductions. Since budgets need to be realistic, if you are reviewing your partner's budget and see that one or more items is too low, that should be pointed out, as well as items that are too high — a difficult move, since it means increasing the budget and expenses! However, it is better to know now what the expenses are likely to be, than to be hit by a surprise in the future.

Again, be careful; it is easy for this activity to get out of hand. Be controlled. Curb your tongue. Avoid personal criticism. Be ready to discontinue the discussion if angers flare. Tread lightly, but rationally. Keep working till you balance the budget, or get the expenses down as far as you can.

A useful technique here is to ask questions rather than make statements that sound like value judgments. Questions like "how did you arrive at that figure?" Or "Is that what we spent in the past?" Will be received more kindly than "You can't do that", "Are you nuts?", "Are you out of your #@&&%$#!! mind?"

How About More Money?
If the budget is in the red to a significant degree and expenses cannot be reduced any further, you'll need to investigate options for increasing family income. If incomes are fixed and cannot be increased through additional training or job change, possibilities include second jobs for one or both spouses, taking in boarders or renting rooms, or doing daycare work. (The latter may be done in the home in situations where the couple has decided that one spouse will continue to be a homemaker to raise very young children). Most localities regulate in-home businesses and daycare facilities; check the rules in your community.

Other options for increasing income include:

• Liquidate one or more of your marital assets (e.g., investments, recreational equipment, collections) and use the proceeds to reduce or eliminate any of the outstanding major debts.

• Take out a loan against an insurance policy, if you have a whole life policy with cash value.

• Take the responsibility for debt payment as part of the financial agreement. (Contact creditors, explain the situation and make arrangements to make minimal payments until you are on a sounder financial basis.)

• Sell the primary residence and allocate some portion of the net proceeds to debt reduction. (Be careful that new rent/mortgage doesn't exceed the old mortgage.)

• Take out a second mortgage or home equity loan to pay down current debt. (Be sure to include the mortgage payments in your budget expenses.) The advantage to this strategy is that home loan interest is a deductible expense at tax time. The disadvantage, of course, is that you put your home at risk should you become unable to meet the required payments.

Money matters are difficult to discuss at the best of times. They are one of the major reasons for family disagreements and problems. In dealing with this area you must be very careful how you communicate with each other and each of you must be free to discontinue the conversation (temporarily) if you become over-anxious or upset.

Negotiating Support Levels

Once the budget has been resolved as much as possible, you'll need to come up with specific support figures. Your first option revolves around negotiating a "whole" support figure (the total amount to be transferred from one partner to the other), and then deciding what proportion, if any, of that general figure is *spousal support* and what proportion is *child support*. The second major option is to begin negotiations for spousal support or child support separately. Either way works well as long as you both are clear on what you are doing. If you and your spouse have agreed not to consider spousal support (alimony) or if you have no children, then consideration need not be given to these areas.

There is an old saying that "you can't get blood out of a stone." It doesn't matter how much one person "wants" a certain amount of support if the other person lacks the resources to pay it. Support amounts need to be based on "ability to pay" as well as need. The reciprocal is also true. That is, just because one person leaves the house each day to earn a living and the other parent stays home to care for the children, doesn't mean that the stay-at-home parent doesn't get support because she or he is not "working." In some families, having one parent stay at home with the children is the primary concern and value, and the parents agree to continue with this model even after divorce. In other families needs and values change. It is not always possible to continue on along the path that was chosen initially. In any event, *this part of the conversation will eventually boil down to "dollars and sense."*

At some point, the partners — on your own or with the help of the mediator — will have to agree to certain amounts for support. Now, you may be saying to yourself, "I don't have to agree to support. If I don't like the amount I am being offered (or asked for) I can always go to court." That's true. It's also true that you can easily spend $25,000 to $60,000 in court and end up paying (or receiving) the same amount. Worse, you could spend that amount and get less or pay more! *Can your family stand the financial strain — not to mention the emotional strain — that court would entail? Keep in mind that going to court could also destroy the positive parenting relationship that the two of you have established in order to care for your children.* I'm not suggesting that you should accept whatever your spouse suggests as "the right amount," nor that you should be pressured into accepting an amount that does not work. Rather, I'm suggesting that the courts really don't know what's best for your family, and that the two of you together (or with the aid of your mediator) can work these issues out the same as you did the issues of parenting and property.

Before we get into the specifics of spousal support and child support, I want to cover another general consideration that affects both. We'll take a look at the details of spousal and child support later in this chapter, but first, let's examine an issue that affects every financial activity: changes in the cost of living — most often showing up as inflation.

Cost of Living Adjustments (COLA)

As you know, things generally get more expensive; they seldom get cheaper. Each year it costs more to purchase the same things. For this reason, many spouses will agree to adjust support payments (after a baseline has been established), in some mutually agreed-upon fashion, to account for changes in the cost of living. There are a number of ways that this can be done. You and your spouse can be quite creative in developing formulas or indexes to help you make cost of living adjustments in support amounts. Some examples include:

• Increasing the support by the CPI — Consumer Price Index — percentage annually. (Call your local public library for current CPI figures.)

• Federal government workers get a certain percentage raise almost every year; some couples have chosen to use the federal cost of living rate.

• A flat percentage increase each year; for example, a two percent or five percent annual increase in the support payment.

• A flat dollar amount increase each year; for example, $5, $10, or $25 per month.

• Other couples tie the cost of living increases into ways that more directly affect the family, such as increases or decreases in family income. For example, if income increases by 5% annually, then the support payment would increase by 5%. This provides a proportional increase in support payments without having all of the increased amount put into support and thereby negating any motivation to earn more money. Uncle Sam, of course, will take a chunk of any increased income to either spouse, so the balance is not quite as lopsided as it may seem.

• Predictable increases or decreases in family expenses may trigger changes in support for some families. Special schools or college for the children can significantly increase expenses (see chapter 8). Discontinuance of day care, coming into an inheritance or insurance benefit may completely reverse the financial picture.

Sarah's income was greater than Neal's, but neither made a lot of money. Additionally, neither was expecting a salary increase nor job promotion soon. It was clear that if Neal were going to make more money he was going to have to work harder (put in more hours, change jobs, or perhaps find a second job). They agreed that Sarah would pay spousal support to Neal, however they quickly saw that if they deducted a dollar of support for every new take-home dollar Neal earned, there would be no motivation for him to work harder. No matter how hard he worked under such a plan, he would have the same amount of money (up to the limit of spousal support). Rather, the couple decided to reduce Neal's support payment by one dollar for every two dollars of net increase he earned. It that way both partners would benefit by Neal's energies. If his income increased to the point where it matched Sarah's, spousal support would no longer be necessary.

Some couples agree that adjustments downward can also be made if an individual either loses work (through no fault of her/his own) or has to take less income to maintain work.

Many couples put a "ceiling" or "floor" on the percentage increase or decrease by which support can be changed in any given year. For example, a spouse who is working one job gets a second job of equal income. It may not be fair to have that individual double the support payment because his or her income has doubled. A ceiling of 5%, 10%, 15%, or 25% increase (or decrease) may be appropriate. In this way, individuals are motivated to go out and develop additional income without feeling that all of it will be turned over to the family without the option of personal use. In this example, of course, we are not talking about "just trying to make ends meet." There are situations where a second job is warranted just to develop enough income for the family's survival.

Any of the above options, and many others, can work. It is up to the couple to pick or create one that feels right, seems reasonable and workable, is not too complex nor difficult to understand or calculate, and will not place an undue burden on them in future years.

Child Support

The amended budgets show the predicted cost of child care for both of you. The figures at the bottom of each "children" column, when added together, indicate the total predicted cost of supporting the children. Separately, those figures indicate each spouse's own projected expenses toward that end. If there is much difference between you in projected expenses or individual income, you'll need to resolve how much (usually) the higher-income spouse will provide to the lower-income spouse for financial support of the children.

(Remember, we are talking about financial support here; I recognize that "child support" goes well beyond the transfer of money, it includes all the love, affection, attention and time one invests in one's children to raise them in the best way possible. This discussion is limited to the financial aspects of support.)

Where possible, both spouses should attempt to have some financial input into child support so that both can feel that they are making a contribution in all areas. However, in family situations where it is agreed that one spouse will stay home to raise young children (or take care of disabled children), it is obvious that the other, employed spouse will have to provide all of the financial support.

There are, in my opinion, no useful formulas for figuring out child (see Child Support Guidelines, p. 110) or spousal support amounts. Rather, if the budget has been prepared appropriately and discussed rationally, common sense will dictate what support amounts are needed.

Helen and Richard had worked on their budgets for quite some time, but had some difficulty when it came to cost of clothing for the children. Richard had not spent much time buying clothes for the children and felt that the amount Helen proposed for clothing purchases was exorbitant; he resisted her budget proposal because of those figures. Although Helen was able to produce receipts for recent expenses, Richard was still resistant. The couple ended up taking clothing for the children out of the budget, deciding to handle its as a separate issue. They were then able to arrive at and resolve a transfer of funds based on the remaining budget.

In the follow-up discussion of clothing, Richard and Helen agreed to take equal responsibility, proposing to meet at the beginning of each school semester and the summer to discuss clothing needs and to decide which parent would be responsible for purchasing particular items. Both were free to purchase additional clothing on their own. They would discuss as a separate issue any unusual or special items that might be requested (e.g., prom dress, band uniform, athletic apparel).

This approach accomplished several positive things at one time: they resolved the budget; they set up mechanisms for some reality-based negotiations with regard to the children's clothing; and they provided each parent some quality contact time with the children, shopping for clothing.

Child Support Guidelines

Since the first edition of this book was published in 1987, a number of changes have taken place across the country with regard to child support. Most states now have published "child support guidelines." These guidelines vary from state to state. Most are available on the Internet (search under "child support guidelines" for the latest information).

In the beginning, the child support guidelines were used by the court to calculate child support in contested cases only. The guidelines were originally discretionary. That is, the judge could choose to use the guidelines or come up with his own amount. In various states, this has changed to make the guidelines mandatory. That is, the judge is bound to use the guidelines to calculate child support when the case reaches court. In some states (Maryland, for example) the guidelines are supposed to be mandatory, even where the case is not contested. That is, the court is bound to review the separation or divorce document to make sure that the child support closely approximates the state child support guidelines, even when the entire process is voluntary (non-adversarial). This is more than a little disconcerting for parents who believe they know what's best for the family, financially as well as in other ways, and are told by the state that they must abide by the child support guidelines.

You might begin to think, from this information about state child support guidelines, that there is no point in developing a budget for child support. This is not true. In fact, it's more important than ever. Child support guidelines are developed by accountants and actuaries (both very nice types of people) who calculate child support amounts, amounts based on estimates, averages, and consumer information. These numbers are then applied universally, regardless of the standard of living of the people involved. In some cases this means that people who have a higher standard of living and can afford to pay more don't have to, and people with a lower standard of living are asked to pay more than they can afford. In a few cases that I have seen, paying child support according to guidelines places families at greater risk than not paying.

By using budgets, you'll be able to see what the real expenses are for your family. You can then compare the amounts that you calculate with your state's child support guidelines. Based on this, you may choose to pay more than the child support guidelines index suggests (the guidelines do not preclude overpayment). If the child support guidelines are more than the family can afford, you may want to look at how things can be adjusted, or develop a rationale to present to the court why child support is proposed to be less than the guidelines require.

I remind you again: this can be a very ticklish and difficult area to discuss. You and your partner should be especially careful in your manner of communication. There may be a tendency for the partner earning more money to feel used because he or she must transfer money for support. The spouse bringing in less money may feel diminished, less powerful and less in control because she or he has relatively lower income and will be receiving money from the other spouse. Most people I work with don't like the idea of receiving support, regardless of their situation. All of these feelings tend to invoke angry and hostile responses that get in the way of good communication. (Remember , if either of you becomes emotionally upset, postpone any discussions that you may be having before things get out of hand.)

Once a child support figure is reached, a number of other issues need to be discussed with regard to child support, including:

- How long the child support will continue?
- How will the child support be adjusted?
- Will there be cost of living increases or decreases?
- What about special expenses?
- Where there is more than one child, will termination of support vary according to the ages of the children or some other event?

Length of Time — Many couples assume that child support is discontinued at age 18, the point at which children reach the age of majority. While this may be appropriate for some families, it is important to remember that some children may still be in high school after they turn age 18. Whatever the reason, the child is in school, living at home, and being supported by one or both parents. There may need to be a written understanding between you and your spouse that support will continue as long as this needed schooling continues. (There are certain special situations that must be accommodated. For example, most court settlements have provisions for parents to continue child support indefinitely for children with certain handicapping conditions. College is another consideration, and is discussed separately in chapter 8.)

Special Expenses — You may wish to reach agreement with your partner concerning how special or exceptional expenses — those which fall outside of normal budgetary coverage — will be handled. Such expenses might include an automobile or automobile insurance for an older child, special clothing, a field trip, vacation time, or camp. It is sometimes possible to predict what special or exceptional expenses will occur; some couples simply say that if special expenses do occur they will negotiate them as they come up. Others want to define what "special expenses" means, and make a list of the types of expenses that they are willing to discuss.

It is helpful to agree on a formula for coverage of special expenses beforehand. While the options are open and unlimited, some couples I've dealt with have chosen to split special expenses evenly, others proportionally to income, and others in a ratio that feels okay to them, although it may not reflect any obvious proportion or formula. Some families require, depending on the circumstance and age of the child, that the child put up some of the money, through work or an existing savings account.

Termination — A key issue that needs to be resolved in regard to adjusting child support is the time and manner in which it will be ended. As we have already mentioned, there are certain considerations for deciding how long it will run. If there is only one child, when those considerations or milestones (e.g.. age 18 or graduation from high school) have been met, obviously it is a simple task to discontinue. If there is more than one child, however, the couple will need to discuss in what proportion the allotment will be reduced as each child reaches the milestone. For some families, simply dividing the support amount by the number of children is an answer. For others, reducing the amount by less than a full share allows some relief for the paying spouse but also some additional margin and benefit for the younger children. (It may be argued that the cost of a single child is more than half the cost of two children, since some expenses of being a parent are constant, regardless of the number of children at home. For example, when the oldest child turns 18, graduates and moves out, the family should not be expected immediately to move to a smaller house, yet the cost of the larger house continues!)

Dustin and Diane were able to work out the amount of child support relatively easily, but they were undecided about how the support would be discontinued over time. Their children were spread out in ages (14, 8, and 3). How would they provide for the children's education? Where would the children stay during high school? Dustin and Diane ended up agreeing to reduce child support as each child turned 18 or graduated from high school (whichever occurred later). Since there were three children, the support would be reduced by one-third when the first child graduated or turned 18, then the remainder would be reduced by one-half when the second child graduated or turned 18. It would be discontinued when the youngest reached that milestone. Both parents were interested in college for the children, but set aside college support plans to negotiate separately.

Spousal Support

Spousal support, like child support, refers to a number of issues, all of which must be considered in arriving at a fair and equitable agreement between you and your spouse. Spousal support should be based upon the needs of all parties concerned, as demonstrated by a reasonable budget; it must be tempered by current actual income of both spouses, as well as realistic predicted potential incomes.

You've prepared and resolved a budget as described earlier in this chapter. Your next step is to set up guidelines and understandings to cover spouse expenses, similar to those you developed in the child support section. You and your spouse need to agree on the starting amount of spousal support, how long it will last, and under what conditions it will change, if any. In general, it is understood that spousal support will be transitional in nature (that is, it will last only as long as necessary to help the receiving spouse become independent.). There are some exceptions, however, depending on age, health, education, work experience, and length of marriage. The base amount for spousal support is negotiated by comparing the bottom lines of the "husband" and "wife" *expense* columns on the "adjusted" budget chart with anticipated *income*, after considering expenses for child support (if any)

> **Cam made more money than Nolan** and accepted the reality that she would have to pay some support to him. However, Nolan expected a salary increase in the coming year, and he was being considered for promotion within the company as well. Since these income increases were likely, the couple agreed to reduce the amount of support Cam paid by an amount equal to Nolan's net take-home pay from the salary increases (and from the promotion, if it came through).

Again, the reminder that talking about financial matters is extremely difficult for many couples; you may need to tread lightly (but firmly) in this area. It is not unusual for a spouse making significantly more money to feel angry and abused at the thought of having to provide financial support for a number of years to someone with whom he or she will no longer be living or interacting on a regular (or perhaps friendly) basis. This is particularly true when the separation or divorce was not that spouse's idea in the first place. Conversely, the spouse in need of support may feel hurt, angry, embarrassed, and frustrated at not being self-sufficient and able to care of his or her own needs. This is especially true for someone who was interested in working outside the home and was asked/told not to.

In general, it is safe to say that spouses on "both sides of the coin" are upset with the idea of having to deal with support issues. Those who pay are fearful that they may not be able to meet their own needs if they are required to pay support; those who receive support are afraid that they might be dependent, or perhaps will not be able to meet their own needs even with support.

If you are able to see this as a transition period, the time in which you and your spouse are willing to work together (although living apart) in order to facilitate your financial and emotional independence, you will find the task more readily accomplished. The outcome is not always satisfactory. Sometimes, the best a couple can do is to discuss and negotiate to the point where support is acceptable to both of them and both feel they can "live with" the arrangement.

Do not expect the outcome here to make either of you "happy."

> **Jim and Kim** agreed that a temporary or "rehabilitative" alimony was required for them. They agreed that Jim would pay Kim $500 a month in spousal support for the first year. Beginning in the second year, the spousal support amount would be decreased by $25 a month every three months; thus, at the end of the second year Kim would be receiving $400 per month. The payments would decrease $25 per quarter for the next four years, until no further support payment was paid.

When discussing basic levels of spousal support, you will want to compare projected monthly expenses with monthly net income. However, it is appropriate to set up contingencies to cover projected increases (or decreases) in income by either spouse, and how those increases (or decreases) will affect the support payment.

For example, if you and your partner have agreed that you will transfer $200 per month at current income levels, and the expectation is that your partner's take home income is going to increase by $100 a month, you may want to discuss reducing the amount of support. Not necessarily dollar for dollar, since that would prove of little motivation for your partner to gain extra income, but you might agree to reduce the support by $1 for every additional $2 brought in (remember Neal and Sarah on page 106). Thus, you'd be paying $150 instead of $200 (the original $200 less half your partner's $100 increase). This formula would help your partner to be motivated to work toward developing additional income.

Another variation is to discuss the possibility of decreasing payments over time (in increments) based on overall gross income. For example, if you make $20,000 and your spouse makes $40,000, it may be appropriate to decrease the support payment by 25 percent when your income reaches $25,000: 50 percent when you're income reaches $30,000 and so on. If your spouse's income is increasing (or decreasing!), that may be considered. Keep in mind that these proposals are all relative. A lot depends on the absolute needs of each family member and everyone's income. Remember also, that if (in the example above) your spouse earns $40,000 a year and pays you $10,000 a year on top of the $20,000 you earn, then in reality that two of you have almost the same income $30,000 (exclusive of tax implications).

> **Mike and Margaret** didn't want to be bothered with comparing net dollars frequently, but agreed to share information about gross income once a year (at tax time). They worked out this formula: for every $2000 increase in Margaret's gross income, Mike would reduce his support payment to her by $100 a month for the next twelve months. They also agreed to a ceiling: if Margaret's income reached $24,000, support would be discontinued altogether.

Discontinuance — How long will spousal support last? You will need to talk with your spouse about the period of anticipated spousal support and how it will be discontinued. In families where both spouses have potential to earn income, there is the expectation that each individual will try to gain independence in a "reasonable" amount of time. Options include:
• pick a cut-off date of a certain number of months or years in the future;
• continue the support payment for a certain number of years, then taper off the payment (by either a specific dollar amount, an agreed percentage, or until a certain amount of time has gone by);
• provide residential care until the children reach a certain age or milestone in school, then either discontinue or taper off accordingly. It is also possible for couples to leave the length of support open-ended, specifying a point or points in time to renegotiate the support amount.

Although support is often looked upon as transitional or rehabilitative, this is not necessarily automatic. Couples that have been married for a long time, with one spouse who has never worked and has little vocational potential, may agree that support will go on for an extended period. Some couples discontinue support when the pension account is activated and pension funds are paid to both parties (again, this is not automatic).

Emotional Considerations — There are no right or wrong answers to the questions of spousal support. *Support seldom feels good either to the person providing the support or to the person receiving the support.* Rather, the best a couple can do is to discuss and negotiate to the point where support is acceptable to both of them and they both feel they can "live with" the arrangement.

The emotional response most of us have to financial concerns ranges from uncomfortable at best to sheer panic in the extreme case. And divorce is not "the best" of circumstances.

There are times, when support is not needed from a financial standpoint (both partners are working, or the property division will provide more than enough income for independence) where support is still appropriate. *These are situations in which the support says "thank you" or "I appreciate the time that we had together."* This support is an "acknowledgment" of the value of the other person even at a time (or perhaps especially at a time) when the partners are going in different directions. There is nothing wrong with this type of support as long as it fits into the overall financial picture.

Spousal support offers yet another challenge to a couple's creativity. Successful support negotiations require that both spouses look at support in terms of fairness. Financial resources must be shared equitably, according to the needs of both parties, not according to who gets more or less money. In this area, perhaps more than any other, you may need the services of a trained mediator to help you discuss the issues.

If you or your spouse have trouble with any of the issues in this chapter, contact a mediator for help.

"Homework" for the Insurance Discussion

Both partners should complete each assignment in writing prior to the discussion of this topic. Bring the written work to the session. When "several" items are suggested, prepare two or more.

Reading — Read chapter 7, "Insurance" before completing the following assignments. Read and follow the Agenda for this topic provided in Appendix A.

Life Insurance — Make a list of all your life insurance policies, term or whole life, group or individual, on all members of the family. Include the face value and cash value (if any).

Health Insurance — Make a list of all your health insurance policies, group or individual, covering all members of the family. Check the levels of coverage (100%, 80%, ...). Check the cost of premiums for individual policies through employers and other sources. Consider who will be responsible for covering children and how uninsured medical/dental/psychiatric expenses will be covered.

Policy Maintenance — Prepare several alternative approaches for handling current policies, obtaining new policies, eliminating unwanted policies, protecting current policies, and discontinuing policies at appropriate times.

7

Insurance
It's A Matter of Policy

THE NEXT FEW SECTIONS (and chapters) may seem somewhat brief; that's because they are. If you and your spouse have come this far in the decision-making process, discussion about these issues should be quick and easy for you. Additionally, these are areas in which the mechanics of how goals are achieved (term vs. whole life insurance, health insurance vs. membership in an HMO, what type of college, how to file income taxes, ...) is too much an individual choice to cover all the options here. There are some technical issues that need to be addressed, and some of the decisions are best made only after independent research and/or discussion with a trained expert.

Don't misunderstand: I am not suggesting you ask an "expert" what you and your spouse *should do*, only that you get expert help in *how* to go about doing what you decide. The areas discussed here which require such help are "insurance" (this chapter's topic), "college" (chapter 8), and "taxes" (chapter 9).

The two basic types of insurance most couples are concerned about are *life* and *health*. *Disability* insurance is also a consideration, and will be dealt with briefly as well.

Life Insurance
Few separating couples see far enough into the future to plan for insurance needs, so let's take a look ahead and consider that now.

Assume you and your spouse have decided on spousal and/or child support, and have arranged joint responsibility for paying off marital debts. You draft a separation agreement and sign it. Now all your "stuff" is separate and you begin to function based on the money that is transferred. Then the one paying support dies suddenly. There's the survivor, counting on support for the children and perhaps for himself or herself, and the support suddenly disappears. Even if support were not an issue, resolution of marital debt might be. How does the survivor carry on? (It could be you.)

For separating couples, life insurance is one way of assuring that financial promises made and responsibilities assumed can be carried out, even in the event of the untimely demise (if we are involved, it's always untimely) of one partner. Each of us has different feelings about life insurance. I'm not trying to sell you on the idea of what type of insurance, if any, you should have. If the two of you have agreed to child support, spousal support, or the responsibility of large marital debts (mortgages, credit cards, tuition), there are expenses which need to be covered. If you or your spouse dies, most of those expenses will still exist. That's where insurance comes in.

If you accept the idea of using life insurance as a backup (safety net) for support payments (or other debts), you'll want to look at what the payments will be in order to determine if you have a large enough safety net (life insurance coverage).

How Much Do You Need?
The first step is to estimate the total amount of support that will be required. To do this, multiply the number of months that support will be paid by the monthly dollar amount of support projected. The result is the total amount that is projected to be paid out over the period of support. We'll use an example to examine several options for how such a situation might be handled.

Mr. and Mrs. Endit have agreed to a support payment of $100 per month for 20 years. The Endits have also agreed to a cost of living increment tied to Mr. Endit's yearly income increase (he'll be paying support to her). Additionally the couple agreed that Mr. Endit would pay the mortgage on the house in which Mrs. Endit was living (Please note that $100 is not being *recommended* as a support payment, but is chosen to make calculations simple in the example. An actual support payment could be many times that amount. Adjust your calculations accordingly.)

As a first step, multiply the $100 monthly payment by 12 (months/year) by 20 (years). The result is the total amount to be paid over 20 years: $24,000. They then added in the $50,000 still outstanding for the mortgage on Mrs. Endit's house, bringing the total up to $74,000. This was the amount of life insurance that they agreed that Mr. Endit would carry. (This figure does not include any consideration for changes due to cost of living or other modifications, but the amount can be adjusted if you project such changes).

Where Does the Money Come From?

There are several possible ways to structure a life insurance program to insure funding of support. Let's take a look at some of the possibilities.

Plan A. One way of approaching the issue is simply to purchase an insurance policy on Mr. Endit's life, with a face value of $74,000. This approach is used by some couples because of its simplicity. While it does end up being slightly more expensive, it also has a built-in cost of living factor. That is, for each month Mr. Endit continues to live, the payoff amount ($74,000) is greater than the remainder needed to cover the actual support balance ($73,900 after one month, $72,800 after one year, etc.) Some look at this difference as a cost of living increase factor; the support payments might actually have been adjusted upward if he lived and his salary increases had continued as expected.

Plan B. Another approach is to determine the amount of money the Endits would need to invest in order to develop "interest" equivalent to the support payments. That amount can be the face value of a life insurance policy. The assumption here is that the cash proceeds of the policy would be invested in some type of interest-bearing account, and the interest would be used to make the monthly support payments. At the end of the support period the remaining principal can be returned to Mr. Endit's estate, passed on to the children for their education, or handled in some other way. For the Endits, this might mean an insurance amount of $50,000, with the expectation that the money would be invested in an account earning an average 8% interest. Such an account would produce about $4000 dollars a year ($100/month for support and $233 for the mortgage). At the end of the allotted time the principal would still be intact and could be used for any agreed purpose. As you can see, the face amount of insurance needed for covering the Endit's support agreement in this second example is smaller and therefore less expensive. (You will note that in this option there is no provision made for cost of living change).

Plan C. Still another approach is to set up a policy that provides a lump sum up front, which will be deposited or invested. A combination of interest and principal will then provide the necessary support. The amount is calculated so that at the end of the support period there will be nothing left in the account to assign (in contrast to Plan B above). To provide $100 a month for 20 years for Mrs. Endit's support and $233 for the mortgage would require a face amount of around $35,000, assuming it is invested at 6% upon Mr. Endit's death. In this plan, the support payments are made up of a combination of interest and principal paid out each month. This approach does not provide for cost of living or inflation increases, however, and at the end of 20 years, there would be no money left. This approach is called purchasing an "annuity". As can be seen it is somewhat less expensive but requires the money up front to buy the annuity.

Plan D. The next approach is to use what is called "decreasing" life insurance. In this type of policy the face value decreases over time (set over almost any period you choose) so that the payoff at the end of the term is $0. This may seem an ideal solution and for some it may be. The assumption in this case is that the longer Mr. Endit lives, the lower the total support amount will be, since the monthly payments to Mrs. Endit and the mortgage company will be made for fewer years. Thus a decreasing amount of insurance is needed to protect the plan. Decreasing life insurance has a level premium, and I have been told that it is not always as cost-effective as it seems. (In the last years, for instance, the premium for almost no insurance coverage is the same as it was in the beginning for full coverage.)

Plan E. The next approach is to calculate the amount of coverage necessary, as above, and select that as the death benefit. As time goes on, and the spouse whose life is covered continues to live (we hope), that person can shift beneficiary status to someone else, as long as enough protection is maintained to cover the outstanding promise of payment.

One more thing to keep in mind when trying to come up with an appropriate amount of insurance coverage: you may want to include in your calculations the cost of paying off outstanding credit card debts and/or funding advanced education (college) for the children or the surviving spouse. In the next chapter we'll talk more about additional education.

I would caution you to check with an insurance expert, your CPA, or a qualified financial planning specialist before you choose any approach.

More Life Insurance Questions

Should you buy term life insurance or whole life insurance policies? How long should the policies be in effect? How can you protect yourself and your spouse to make sure the policies are maintained and the beneficiaries are not changed? Should the surviving spouse, or the children, be named as beneficiary? Some of these questions I can help you with now, others will require you to do some research on your own. (Start with the resources listed in the Appendix.)

The first thing you have to do is look at what you have. Are there already existing life insurance policies on either spouse? Do you have any personal policies — bought through an agent or directly from the insurance company? (You're probably aware of any whole life policies; they generally have cash value, which should have been considered when you were discussing the division of marital property.) What about group (term) policies through work or an association?

If you have no life insurance now, is any available through your employer? You may be able to sign up and purchase very inexpensive (usually term) life insurance at work. Be aware that employer sponsored plans often (though not always) terminate when/if you change jobs.

If there is life insurance, what is the face value — the amount that will be paid if the insured person dies? How does this amount (or these amounts, if you have more than one policy) compare with your strategies or plans for setting up a protection system for support, as mentioned above?

If you need additional life insurance, you're going to need to contact your employer's personnel office, an insurance agent, or an insurance company that sells direct (i.e., by mail or via the Internet). Just as a frame of reference, you should know that, as of this writing (2000), a 45-year-old man in good health can get

$100,000 dollars worth of group term life insurance for approximately $186 a year ($15.50/month). Keep in mind that the premium for that amount of coverage does increase over time, but that is the current starting rate. (It may also interest you to know that this is down from $250 in 1987).

A carefully-considered life insurance plan will take into account both spouses, especially when there are children. Remember that both incomes are part of the child support budget. If either of you dies, the children's needs will continue and the expense to the surviving parent is likely to increase (even to the parent who was paying support).

Term or Whole Life? A lot depends on your financial situation. Generally speaking, whole life (a.k.a. universal life, comprehensive life) insurance is more expensive than term life insurance and requires a greater outlay of cash, perhaps at a time when funds are quite tight. Such policies do build up cash value in addition to the face value, and thus become something of a "forced savings" plan, but usually at lower than prevailing interest rates. Keep in mind that you primarily are looking for *protection* for the support agreement, not an *investment* vehicle.

Termination. How long should the life insurance be kept in effect? Consider how long support (or other) payments are expected to continue. Many couples agree to continue life insurance in effect (at a minimum) until the support payments are discontinued; others agree to maintain the insurance for longer — or shorter — periods, depending on their needs and financial situation.

Payment of Premiums. In some cases, the spouse with the greatest earning power pays the insurance premiums. In other situations, the person whose life is covered by the insurance pays the premium. (Of course, these are often the same person.) Some couples also set up a provision that allows the beneficiary spouse to make payments to insure that they are made in a timely fashion, and to continue payment of the premiums, at his or her option, after the agreed termination date.

Protection from Changes in the Policy. A moment for a sad tale... George and Marilyn worked out an agreement (not in mediation) which provided for insurance coverage as a back-up to support. When George died in an accident four years later, Marilyn expected to receive some insurance money to help provide for the children. The insurance company told Marilyn that the policy had been canceled more than two years before George's death. The couple had not set up any protection for the beneficiary to guard against such an occurrence. "Ah ha!" you say, "There was a divorce contract." Right you are. So what! If the money didn't exist in the estate (which it didn't) then where was it to come from? You can't sue someone who is dead. If you and your spouse are going to consider using insurance to provide back-up to your joint support system, you may also want to consider protecting the system. Here's how one couple did that.

A young couple with three young children, **Dan and Loretta** recognized that while they were in good health now, they might not be so fortunate in the future. They also recognized that neither their assets nor their estates were very substantial. They agreed to safeguard Dan's support payments to Loretta by a life insurance policy with a face value of $100,000. Dan would be responsible for the premiums, but Loretta would own the policy. Even though they trusted each other and recognized that they each had a commitment to co-parenting, they also recognized that people's feelings and circumstances change over time. They were trying to build a safety factor into the agreement that would preclude a change of beneficiaries on the insurance policy, a situation that might not be discovered until it was too late. Since Loretta owned the policy, she would be immediately notified if Dan ceased payment on the premiums or tried to have the beneficiaries changed. Named as beneficiary was a trust for the children, with Loretta as trustee, and with the understanding that the money would be used for the children's upbringing and college education. A $50,000 insurance policy on Loretta's life was added as well, with Dan the owner and a similar trust (with Dan as trustee) as beneficiary, to use for the children in their upbringing and education should Loretta die.

With regard to protection, there are several options available to most couples. Where the policies are privately owned (not group coverage), it is possible to make the owner of the policy also the beneficiary. The owner controls whose name is placed as beneficiary and makes sure that the premiums are paid. (This does not necessarily mean that the owner must actually *pay* the insurance premiums.)

For example, you and your spouse may agree that there should be an insurance policy on each of you. You could agree to each own a policy on the other's life, with either you or the children as beneficiary. With you as owner of the policy, you do not have to worry that the policy will be discontinued without your knowledge, or that the beneficiary of the policy will be changed. You may each still be responsible for paying the premium on the policy on your own life, but if either of you discontinued premium payments, the owner would be notified and have the option of paying the premium and maintaining the policy. The owner could then inquire of the other spouse to find out why the premium was not paid.

Joint ownership of privately owned insurance policies is also a possibility that you may wish to consider, if your situation warrants.

In some cases, owning (or co-owning) the policy on your spouse's life is not possible, either because it is a business or group policy, or because of a pre-existing condition in setting up the policy. If this is the case, you still have an option for protection. This requires contacting the insurance company, after appropriate discussion with your spouse, and having the beneficiary (whoever may have been decided upon) labeled as "irrevocable beneficiary." While this does not mean that the beneficiary on a policy can't be changed, it does mean that whoever is noted as the "irrevocable beneficiary" will be notified if changes in beneficiary status are made. That person can also be notified if the policy is discontinued (allowed to lapse). If you are the "irrevocable beneficiary" on your spouse's policy, your spouse cannot change the beneficiary or discontinue the policy without your knowledge. The same is true for policies on your life in which your spouse is "irrevocable beneficiary."

Bernadette and Doug both agreed that they wanted an insurance policy to safeguard continuation of the support payments. Luckily, since finances were tight, each had a life insurance policy provided through their employment. Since they were group term life insurance policies, the couple could not assign ownership of the policies as a protection for notification and change. They found that they could, however, assign "irrevocable beneficiary" status to the primary beneficiaries. Since each was the "irrevocable beneficiary" on the other's policy, that person would be notified if the insured person tried to change the beneficiaries on the policy. The notification allowed them, if necessary, to remind each other of their agreement to maintain the life insurance, or coverage "of an equivalent amount." Since they were both young and might not stay with their current employers forever, the phrase "of an equivalent amount" gave them flexibility to acquire coverage elsewhere without violating the terms of the separation agreement.

All of this may sound quite complicated (it is), and needless (it's not). There will be a written agreement between you (which is a legally binding contract), which can state that you will each keep such policies in force. However, without these protections you may find out too late that the agreement was not carried out. *The use of cross ownership or irrevocable beneficiary helps reduce the possibility of unknown changes or discontinued policies.*

Non-Insurance Protection
While insurance can be an effective back-up for support, you may be among those who are opposed to the use of insurance. There is another approach you and your partner can use if there is a fairly substantial estate. In such a case you can provide — through your separation agreement, divorce contract or will — to continue financial responsibility from your estate. You and your spouse will need to set up a formula for how much and how long the estate

will provide support. The information on how this will occur should be recorded along with all the other tentative decisions made up to this point.

> **Barry and Terry** worked out their situation regarding coverage of the support payment without using life insurance. Each was relatively well off financially because of money that had been left by rich relatives. They agreed that, rather than set up life insurance policies, they would simply arrange for the appropriate amounts of money from their estates to be left in trust for the children — or paid to the other spouse for care of the children — in event of their deaths while the children were under 18 or in college. In that way, if Barry died, an amount equal to his remaining obligation of support would be paid to Terry for use in raising the children, since they lived with her. Similarly, if Terry died, and the children were to live with Barry, funds from her estate would be set aside for child-rearing expenses, education, health care, travel.

Health Insurance and Health Coverage

Another insurance issue for separating couples is coverage for the health and medical expenses of the partners and the children, including dental and psychiatric needs. Many families have health insurance policies through employers, individual plans, or equivalent coverage in a health maintenance organization (HMO). (Far too many have no such coverage, however.)

You will want to discuss with your spouse who is to be responsible (pay the premiums) for health insurance (or equivalent) coverage, and how it will be maintained. Does a health insurance policy (or equivalent) currently exist? Is it available through work? What happens if the employed spouse leaves that job? (Transportability of coverage is becoming a universal standard, but there are exceptions, and there may be additional costs for the employee and family members.) What care does the health insurance policy cover? What percentage of medical expenses is covered?

Is An Ex-Spouse Covered? On many health insurance policies, both spouses can be maintained even though they are separated. Usually, in situations of divorce, both spouses are responsible for providing their own health insurance coverage. There is a growing trend for divorced couples to continue on the same policy, but this is not universal. Check with your health insurance representative (e.g., benefits officer or independent agent) if this possibility interests you.

Federal law (COBRA) requires that spouses of employees covered by health insurance have equal access to the same coverage (under certain conditions). This means that if one of you is employed and covered by health insurance, the other can apply for similar coverage at equivalent cost, if certain criteria are met. This insurance is usually cheaper than buying a separate (individual) health insurance policy. The personnel department of the employer should be able to help with this.

Frank and Carolyn had very, very tight budgets. There was very little fluff and it became apparent that if Frank, who had never worked, was going to be covered by medical insurance, the cost of an individual policy — even at minimal coverage — would break the budget. Luckily, they heard about a new law in their state, which required employer-sponsored health plans to offer health insurance coverage at equivalent rates for uninsured, unemployed, divorced spouses of the employees. That is, since Carolyn was covered on a group health insurance policy through her employment, Frank could acquire coverage on the same policy for the same (group) rates that the employees paid. Since it was a large company with a large group, the cost per person for good coverage was considerably less than the cost of an individual policy of lower coverage that Frank would have had to consider. All it took was a call to the personnel department to arrange for the appropriate papers and coverage at the time of the divorce.

Who Covers the Children? If both spouses work, and have access to health insurance at (usually) low cost through their employers, it may be useful to maintain the children on both policies. This is especially helpful where there are children with a history of illness. By maintaining two separate policies, you can (sometimes) negotiate with the various health insurance carriers for coverage of medical expenses and thereby reduce the cost to yourselves. If the employer does not provide medical insurance coverage free, discussion will have to take place about whether it's available, at what additional cost, and how that can be built into the budget. You will want to have some discussion and get some acknowledgment about which parent will ultimately be responsible for maintaining the health insurance coverage.

Jeff and Diane listed all three children on both of their employer-sponsored health insurance policies. Each had a payroll deduction, which reduced their overall cash available. Since the children had histories of illness, and neither policy covered more than 70% of any particular medical cost, the couple was always having to pay out of pocket for about 30% of the children's medical expenses. Rather than continue this, they agreed to continue parallel coverage, billing each insurance company at 50% rather than 70%. Each company was happy for the reduction in cost and was glad to negotiate a maximum coverage of 50% rather than 70%. This gave Jeff and Diane some leeway in terms of the children's medical care, at a cost considerably below what they would have had to pay for uninsured expenses. (Note that some companies are unwilling to negotiate such an arrangement, and will only pay "all or none" of the expense. You'll need to check to see what the policies of your carrier are.)

How Long Will Health Coverage Be Maintained for the Children? These issues are similar to those found in child support, although there are some other considerations. Even though you both may agree to stop child support at a given age (18, for example), you may still be able to continue carrying the children on the health insurance policy or in the HMO until they are older. You may be able to do this much less expensively than they can obtain their own coverage. This is especially true if they are in school (full time). You and your spouse will want to discuss this and decide how it will be handled.

Uninsured Medical Expenses
Once you and your spouse have discussed and decided on health insurance coverage, your task is only half finished. You'll need to determine how the uninsured medical (dental, psychiatric) expenses will be covered. Most health insurance policies and HMO's, while covering a wide variety of problems, do not cover them all — at least not at the 100% level. You and your partner will need to discuss how exceptional medical expenses for your children will be paid. Many couples agree to divide these additional expenses in some fashion. Options include splitting the cost equally, dividing it proportionally to income, dividing it on some other percentage basis or on some other flat dollar amount.

If you have already built medical expense costs into your budget, you may want to consider this amount when going through additional cost negotiations. For example, if $25 a month has been set aside in the children's column for medical costs not covered by insurance, you may wish to discuss how to divide any expenses greater than that ($300 a year) already covered in the budget figures.

When **Bob and Judy** separated, they recognized the importance of finding out which of them had the best and cheapest health care coverage available through their employers. As it turned out, Judy's employer had a very good group plan which cost her nothing directly (there was no payroll deduction), and which covered medical/dental/vision and psychiatric care. They readily agreed that she would be responsible for maintaining coverage for herself and the children; Bob retained his own medical coverage through his employer. That was the easy part. When it became time to discuss how uninsured medical expenses would be paid, the couple had a little difficulty. Since there was no history of medical problems, they did not have a good grasp of what such expenses might be. And since their incomes were not equal they did not feel equally capable of covering a large expense. They each had budgeted a small fund for unexpected uninsured medical expenses (Judy, $20 a month; Bob, $10 a month). They ultimately agreed on a plan to split uncovered health costs for the children: any amount greater than $240 for Judy or $120 for Bob would be split proportionally to the couple's income. For instance, if she incurred a $300 medical expense not covered by insurance, she would pay the first $240, and the remainder ($60) would be divided and paid for proportionally to Bob's and Judy's incomes at the time.

Remember, that though we have talked about "medical" expenses, dental, visual and psychiatric expenses are included in this discussion as well.

Disability Insurance
Disability insurance coverage pays you money when you are physically unable to work. Some policies pay only when you are in the hospital; others pay when you are out of work 15 days, (30, 45, 60, 90, or 180 days), if you meet the criteria set forth in the policy. The amount of payoff depends on how much premium you pay.

Some couples and many financial advisors feel that disability insurance is just as important as life insurance, since it helps defray expenses in situations where the individual is unable to work for medical reasons (being laid off or fired or quitting doesn't count). This type of insurance is generally more expensive than life insurance coverage, but it is useful if you can afford it. (Statistically, you're more likely to be disabled for an extended period than to die while you're still employed.) Many people who are self-employed carry disability insurance. In situations where an employee can save sick days and be paid for extended time off, disability coverage is less cost effective.

Working Out the Details of Protection
I mentioned at the beginning of this chapter that there are a number of technical issues to deal with in accomplishing what you mutually decide to do about insurance protection. After you have tentatively agreed in principle with regard to insurance issues, I suggest you contact an insurance or financial expert for guidance. (Start with the benefits officer of your employer, if any, so you know what's available there.) Simply tell the insurance person or financial advisor what you want to do, and ask for several options on how that can be accomplished. *Don't allow yourselves to be pushed into getting anything you don't want.* If you are unsure (about who should be placed as beneficiary, for example), ask several insurance or financial planning people, so you can get a consensus of opinion before you decide. Remember, they are there to provide service to you.

Remember also to write down what you have discussed and tentatively decided.

Kids as Beneficiaries
One of the decisions around insurance has to do with who will be the beneficiary. It is not uncommon for the parents to say, "Let's make the children the beneficiaries." This can be done, however, I encourage parents to consider the following: some insurance policies will not pay money to minors and will hold the money in trust until they turn 18 (or older, depending on policy structure). This means that (a) the money is not available for expenses of daily living; and (b) when the children turn 18 and get the money, they

can do whatever they want with it (e.g., buy a Corvette and drive off into the sunset, or pay for all their friends to go on a trip to Florida at spring break). One hopes that they will use the money wisely, but hey, they're teenagers. How much can you trust their decision-making?

As you can see, it may be useful to select someone else as the beneficiary of the insurance. It might be the other parent or some other family member (with whom the parent gets along), so that the money can be made available to the surviving parent. Remember, the whole point of the insurance policy is to safeguard the promise of payments which cannot be made upon your demise.

As a safeguard to the safeguard, remember to place instructions in your will (as well as in the separation agreement) as to beneficiary status and use of the money.

If you or your spouse have trouble with any of the issues in this chapter, contact a mediator for help.

"Homework" For The College Discussion

Both partners should complete each assignment in writing prior to the discussion of this topic. Bring the written work to the session. When "several" items are suggested, prepare two or more.

Reading — Read chapter 8, "College" before completing the following assignments. Read and follow the Agenda for this topic provided in Appendix A.

Planning for Children — Consider who needs college, how much advanced education you are willing to support, where the money will come from.

Budgeting for College — Use budgeting procedures similar to those followed in chapter 6, "Support," to develop several alternative financial plans for college funding.

Planning for Spouse Education — Consider whether either partner will need additional education in order to become financially independent. If you expect to ask for such help, prepare a tentative plan (including course work and budget) for your further studies. If you expect to be supporting such a program, write down alternative plans for funding, including limits.

8

Will There Be College?

THE CONCEPT OF PROVIDING SUPPORT FOR COLLEGE (or college equivalent) education extends both to children who may be college bound and to spouses who are in need of additional education to help increase social, vocational, or income potential.

Before we go any further, I need to make it clear that I use "college" as a generic term, covering all types of post-high school instruction, including vocational schools and specific skills training programs, in addition to two-year, four-year, and graduate education. Apprenticeship programs or on-the-job training are not generally included; since the individual is working and receiving an income, such programs do not usually cost additional money. In mediation, many couples want to talk about additional education (college or specific skills training), either for themselves or for their children). Thus, you'll find the term "college education" used throughout this chapter to simplify the discussion.

Choices About College
Let us first look at further education for the children. Not everyone feels the same about additional education, of course. Some people consider it necessary, others feel it is nice, others believe it's okay, and many hold that one can get along perfectly well without it. All of these people are right. College is not for everyone.

Providing for additional education is one way of confirming that things will go on for the children in as normal a manner as possible (even though the marriage will not). For some couples, it is a statement to each other that "We will still be here for the children." For others, it's a statement that "We want the children to have better opportunity than we had." These people feel that additional education is the key to success.

If you are among those who consider college important, there are a number of issues that need to be discussed: What level or levels of education (two-year college, four-year college, graduate school)? Which school? Who will pay the school expenses? What are the expenses? For how long? Under what constraints or controls? What is expected from the student (e.g., scholarships, work, academic performance)? How will the children be protected? How will the parents be protected? Is there to be any limit or maximum amount of support?

Assuming that you both agree that further education is important, you can deal with the issues now, or you can deal with them later. If you elect to postpone this subject, set up a specific date when you will get together to discuss how to handle questions about college. *Keep in mind that if you do not plan and set aside for college now, you may be burdened quite severely by the cost later. Keep in mind also that things may be more difficult to discuss later. If you are getting along (talking/negotiating) now it may be a good idea to "keep going while the going is going".* If you consider and plan now, you can discuss your expectations, make decisions about the future, and make a financial plan.

Some couples feel it is their responsibility to support the children completely, with room, board and tuition while they are in school. Others feel it is important for the children to take some responsibility and that parents should provide only those additional monies needed to make college possible. Still others feel that it is up to the children themselves to make their own financial arrangements, and the parents' role is only to offer encouragement.

If the children are young, it is difficult to know whether or not they are "college material," but you have more time to set aside money to help offset the cost of education later. If the children are older, it is easier to determine whether they are likely to go on to school; however, you have a shorter time to accumulate the financial resources needed to provide a complete college education.

Keep in mind also, the enormous value of investing early to pay for education later. The compounding of interest on even the most conservative investments is remarkable. The sooner you start — even with small amounts — the larger the fund will be when it is needed.

For those children who have indicated an interest in attending college, but for whom academic success is not assured, parents may wish to set up a "graduated" system. In this method, parents acknowledge financial responsibility for a two-year (community college) program, and agree to additional support as each level of college (four-year university, graduate school) is completed successfully. Others make a financial commitment only as long as the children maintain passing grades (C or better, B or better, etc.).

> **Leslie and Florence** developed a set of milestones, agreeing that they would pay for their children's education at a two-year community college. If the children were successful, they could go on to a four-year school, and the parents would split the equivalent of state tuition there. Upon successful completion of four years, if any of the children chose to go on to graduate school, Leslie and Florence would split the cost of tuition in proportion to their incomes, after first deducting any grants, stipends or loans made available to the child.

How Much Will It Cost?

Here's another sad story. It's about a couple who, in their separation agreement, agreed to provide financial assistance for their child's college education. Rather than being specific, they made general comments about "paying for the child's education" and "doing everything in their power to provide an education." When the time came to send the youngster to college, they were both financially trapped. They could not support him in the school that he chose to attend. The young man obtained legal counsel and sued the parents for the right — and support — to attend college! Ultimately, the boy won in court, and the parents were forced to liquidate several assets — including the family home — in order to comply with the mandate. Their good intentions came back to haunt them.

Now, you may say to yourself, "This would never happen to me. My children would never do that to me." Probably not, but my guess is that the parents in this story said the same thing. It can't hurt to be careful in this area; protect yourself, your spouse and your children with precise language in your agreement. If things are going well for you and your spouse when the time comes, you can always provide more funds than are specified in the agreement.

I encourage you to consider, to discuss together, and to write down, limits you may wish to set on the money you're willing to commit for your children's education. Educational and living expenses at a private, four-year college can cost as much as $30,000 a year or more in today's (2000) economy.

Protection

You may wish to specify a maximum dollar amount that you and/or your spouse will put forth yearly for college expenses. Another approach is to say that you will be responsible only for paying the portion you have agreed upon (e.g., half) of "the average rate for room, board and tuition at the state college (or state university) in the state in which the children reside at the time they are old enough to go to college." This way you obligate yourself only to state equivalent expenses. (Consider the language carefully. There is often a large difference between the costs at a nearby state college and those at the major state university campus.) That does not mean that you and your spouse cannot pay more if you choose to and are able, it simply means you are not obligated to do so if you are not able.

Carmen and John had different views about college. John wanted to set asidesome money from the sale of the house, put it in an interest-bearing account or mutual fund, and let it grow until the children were of college age. He projected that if $15,000 were set aside now, in the eight years until their son Darwin went to school, the amount would at least double. Carmen believed that it was important for an individual to feel the importance of a college education by having to work while in school. She suggested that she and John make no commitment about a college education, encourage Darwin in self-sufficiency, and hope that things went well — that he would care enough to work his own way through college. They finally settled on a compromise position. After doing a lot of research, they recognized that even $30,000 might not be very much money toward a college education in eight years. Some schools charge as much as $25,000 or $30,000 today for one year of education, let alone four! They agreed to take $15,000 from the sale of the house and put in a special account that would require both of their signatures for withdrawal. The money was not to be used for anything other than Darwin's college (or equivalent) education. They planned to encourage Darwin to apply for any scholarships, grants, stipends or education loans available to him at the time. After Darwin obtained all such funds, money could be drawn from the joint account for use toward tuition, room, and board, not to exceed the average amount which would be paid at the nearby state college campus. Darwin was free to apply to private as well as public schools, but the education fund would provide only the tuition and expenses equivalent to the nearest state school. Darwin would have to make up the difference on his own if he wanted to go to school anywhere else.

Who Pays?

Who will be responsible for the costs of further education? One or both parents? What is included: Tuition? Room? Board? Books? Toothpaste? Beer? Many parents agree to split college expenses in some fashion, perhaps equally, proportionate to income, or in some other proportion decided upon by mutual agreement. Some couples decide that each will set money aside on a regular basis in an investment account for the children's education.

Other couples simply acknowledge responsibility for "coming up with the money" at the appropriate time. When the family home or other assets are being liquidated in a divorce or separation, some parents agree to invest a portion of the profit from those assets to be used for the children's education. Any unused portion can then go either to the children or be returned to the parents.

> Jan and Mike were convinced that their son, Jack, would never make it in college. He had no college ambitions, his grades had not been particularly good and, in fact, he wasn't particularly thrilled with school in general. He did seem to have a talent for mechanical repair, especially automotive repair. They agreed that if and when Jack graduated from high school, if he was interested, he could attend the two-year program at the local automotive training school. They agreed to share equally the cost of that program.

There are now a number of tax-saving college fund plans provided in some states and by some colleges and universities. What you choose to do will depend to a certain extent on where you live. It is possible in some states, for example, to pre-pay state college tuition when a child is young, and be guaranteed full credit for that payment when and if the child enrolls. (Such plans do not guarantee admission, however! The youngster must still qualify academically.) If you are going to pursue one of these plans you will (both) want to do a fair amount of research and preparation. There are books and web sites that can help. I suggest you consult a financial planner, accountant, and college financial aid office for more information or help with this topic.

How is the Money Used?

If you are planning to put money aside, have already put money aside or are lucky enough to have relatives who have established an educational fund, there are several questions and issues you will want to consider and discuss. How will the money be apportioned between the children and for each child? Let's say you have (or plan to have) $50,000 for two children, now ages 10 and 15. How much will go to each child? Will it be 50/50 or some other proportion, since you will still have an additional five years for the younger child to catch up financially? Regardless of the proportions, how much of each child's share can be used each year? Will you use 25 percent, assuming four years of undergraduate education? Will you set some aside for graduate school? Or will you use a larger portion in the first year or two to reduce the need for having your child work until she or he adjusts to college life? As with everything else, there are no "right" answers. However, if you are working well together now, this would be a good time to try to establish the ground rules for the future. Don't forget, regardless of what goes down on paper now, if you both agree to do something else in the future, it is not likely to be a problem.

College for Spouses

Did one of you support the other in finishing a degree, or starting a business, or establishing a presence in the world of work? Did one partner provide the seed money for the other's small business? Did one keep the family and home together while the other got a career started? If you answered "yes" to any of these questions, perhaps spousal education funding should be part of your separation or divorce discussion.

For some couples, additional education for one of the partners is a way of balancing the earning potential of the spouse making less money. For others, it is a way the higher-earning partner can make a statement of acknowledgment or appreciation for the other's help and support while in school. In either case, it's a way of helping the spouse with less income to become more independent and self-directed (assuming further education or training is what they want).

Keep in mind that additional education is not a requirement of separation and it is not for everybody. Most couples know when further education is appropriate. There may even have been previous discussion about "going back to school" for one of the spouses. Even if there was never any prior discussion about additional education, if there is a demonstrable need, it should be discussed. In some cases it will be apparent that additional formal training will enhance the possibility of movement up the career ladder. In other cases, even if advancement will not result, the acknowledgments and opportunity may still be appropriate.

The issues involved in discussing education for a spouse are the same as those mentioned above for the children. You will want to discuss limits regarding location, cost, and length of program support. You may also wish to discuss the subject of what training program (course work) the attending partner will take, and how it was chosen to enhance the individual's vocational or financial potential. Where funds for the program will come from (some joint account or asset, the other spouse, loans for which one or both spouses take some responsibility) is also an important part of the conversation.

Finally, it must be said that regardless of interest, intent, or desire, family finances must allow support of additional education before it can occur. This does not give license to reject the education out of hand with the statement, "We (I) still can't afford it." What is required here, as with all other areas, is a serious look at the intent, direction, and potential of the family prior to the dissolution of the marriage.

Remember: After you have had your discussion and made your tentative decisions, write down the results.

If you or your spouse have trouble with any of the issues in this chapter, contact a mediator for help.

"Homework" For The Income Taxes Discussion

Both partners should complete each assignment in writing prior to the discussion of this topic. Bring the written work to the session. When several items are suggested, prepare two or more.

Reading — Read chapter 9, "Taxes," before completing the following assignments. Read and follow the agenda for this topic provided in Appendix A.

Exemptions — List several alternatives for how you might deal with exemptions — the "automatic" deductions for yourself and your dependents provided on federal and most state tax returns.

Filing — Consider how you would like to file your income tax returns for the years while you are still legally married.

9

Income Taxes
The Other Sure Thing

MOST OF US ARE NOT TAX EXPERTS. Therefore, this section will be brief and point out only those areas I am confident you'll want to consider. There may be other areas that you will need to look at, depending upon your own situation. You may want to confer with a tax expert to make sure you are covering all of the bases.

Taxable Gains on the Sale of Assets
If you and your spouse are planning to sell some assets, you'll want to look at the possible tax implications. Real estate, stocks, mutual funds, and other investment property will be taxed when it's sold. If you sell it for more than you paid for it, the tax man will "cometh." If you've owned it for more than one year, any profit you make on the sale will be taxed at capital gains rates (currently 20% federal tax). If you've owned it one year or less, the tax bite will be at your individual tax rate for ordinary income (currently 15% to 39.6% — or more if you're really rich, in which case you're tanning in the Bahamas while your lawyers battle out the settlement; you're not reading this book).

Sale of Primary Residence
Good News — The tax rules have changed in ways which benefit most people selling a house. Currently, capital gains is only a concern if the profits from sale of a primary residence exceeds $500,000. Additionally, there is no need to take the profit and roll it over into a new residence to protect it. (In fact, you can't rollover the profits to protect them. If you have a profit of more than $500,000 you will need to pay capital gains on the amount over $500,000). Furthermore, you can do this once every two years. That is, each time you sell a house (that is a primary residence) and

make a profit you can spend the money anyway you like (if the profit is less than $500,000).

Finally, the new law allows you to hold the house in joint ownership for a period of time, then sell the house and treat the profits as though it were a primary residence — even though one of the parties has not been living in the house. The law is not clear about the maximum time one can wait. If you are considering holding the house jointly you will want to do two things. Consider checking with an accountant or the IRS for best estimates of time you can hold the house jointly (keep in mind that putting it up for sale and selling the house are two different things). You'll also want to make sure that the rationale for holding the house jointly (to provide stability for the children or to allow the spouse living in the house time to get on his or her feet) is clearly stated in the separation agreement.

Sale of Stocks, Bonds and Mutual Funds

If you have some market investments that you are going to split in some way, you'll want to be careful about how that is done. If the stocks have increased in value, there may be a substantial taxable gain upon their sale. It's important to note that the "net" value of two different stocks with similar "face" value may be significantly different because of their "basis". Additionally, and of no great surprise to anyone, two stocks with the same "face" value (on a specific day) may change quickly; weeks, or even just days, later, one stock may be substantially more valuable than the other. For these reasons, splitting stocks on the basis of "face" values alone can be chancy.

Two ways to divide stocks are to have the stocks evaluated for net worth (value after taxable gain), then shuffle the portfolio until you get the total values you have negotiated. Another way is to split each stock you hold in the proportion that will give the negotiated outcome. In that way you each end up with the same value proportionally. For example, let's assume you've agreed to split the stocks in the proportion 60/40; one spouse is designated to get 60 percent of each stock, and the other gets 40 percent of each stock. In this way, the taxable gains will be the same relative to each stock.

In some cases you may not be able to divide certain stocks (options) and will want to figure out a way to balance value or share in the profit when the stock is sold. This may require some notification and protections built into the agreement so that the spouse who is not the owner would be notified of any sale of the stock.

A final note of caution regarding valuing and/or selling stocks. You are very likely aware of the wild variations in stock prices and value that have been experienced in the market in recent years. Nobody can predict the future of stock values, and most of us have few if any qualifications to make these calculations. Get some advice in these matters from a trusted broker, your tax advisor, a bank officer, or an accountant. Or do some research on your own. There are dozens of books and web sites that offer such help. Some are better than others, of course. (For instance, try *Sylvia Porter's Money Book* or *25 Myths You've Got to Avoid if You Want to Manage Your Money Right* by Jonathan Clements at the library, or www.money.com — the web site of *Money* magazine — online.)

Tax Exemptions

If you have children, you and your spouse will need to discuss who will claim the tax exemptions for the children. While the IRS has some guidelines for figuring out who is entitled to the deductions if there is a dispute, if there is no dispute, they will allow either parent to take the exemptions — with the permission of the other parent. What they don't want is for both of you to claim the same exemptions in the same year.

Priscilla and Philip agreed that they would alternate their one child as an exemption much as they were alternating the co-parenting schedule. They agreed that Priscilla would take the exemption first. When this occurred would depend on whether they filed a joint or separate return — a decision they would make each year, as long as they were separated but not divorced. In all years that they filed jointly, the exemption would appear on the joint return, and refunds or liabilities would be split proportionally to income. In the first year that they filed separately — whether they were separated or divorced — Priscilla would claim the dependent exemption, with Philip entitled to it the following year. They agreed that if they were still married and filing separately, they would split combined refunds or liabilities in proportion to their income.

Basically, your exemption options are:
- One of you taking the exemptions each year
- Splitting the exemptions (if there are multiple children)
- Alternating the exemptions each year

Your rationale for these decisions may be related to support payments or other factors, however, it may be useful for the spouse earning less money to be able to claim the exemptions at the end of the year in order to make ends meet. This should be balanced against the advantages to the spouse with the higher income taking the exemptions in order to free up more money for support payments.

You can see that there is once again no single "right answer." *The decisions that you make will have to be based on sensitivity to everyone's needs and the best interest of the family.* If you decide to divide up the exemptions (if you have more than one child), it is a good idea to specify by name which parent will claim which child, so there will be no misunderstandings at tax time. Similarly, if you decide to alternate the exemptions each year, you must be clear with regard to who takes the exemptions in which years.

One final note about claiming tax exemptions: In order to satisfy the IRS requirement, it may be necessary for the parent providing living space for the children a majority of the time to sign a form (IRS Form 8332) indicating that it is all right for the other spouse to claim the exemptions (if that is the decision that has been made). Again, you may wish to contact your tax expert for more information.

Income Tax Filing — Separated Couples

The next area that you need to discuss is how income tax forms will be filed for the year(s) prior to your divorce. When you are separated, you have the option of filing "jointly" if you both desire, or "married, filing separately." (In some states, if you are separated and have a decree of separation, then filing in the "single" status may be required.) Filing jointly is generally considered to be advantageous for most families, however new changes in tax laws may change this. You will need to discuss the current tax year, possibly the previous year (if you have not yet filed), and conceivably future years (if neither of you plan to get a divorce in the near future). You cannot file jointly in the year that the divorce actually takes place. Even if you're divorced on December 31st, you still cannot file jointly as a married couple for that year.

There is one more issue that needs to be addressed in filing status and that is the "head of household" issue. When you are separated and filing separately, one spouse (parent) can file separately as "head of household." There is a tax advantage to filing this way. The tax rates are less than filing "separately" but more than filing "jointly." The "head of household" status is given to the person with whom the children stay more often. This is not a reason to ask for more time with the children or to renegotiate the parenting plan. Rather, filing status is mentioned to help you both maximize your savings after all the other decisions have been made.

One way to balance the "head of household" issue is with the "exemption" issue. For the family with average income, where one parent claims head of household and the other parent claims exemptions for the two children, the tax bite is very close to even. This is not to say that one person should always be head of household and the other take the exemptions. There are times when it may be appropriate for the same person to have both. That is for both of you to decide. Remember though, that exemptions can be traded or given up, and head of household is based strictly on time. It seems to me, the only way this could be alternated is in the parenting plan, with the children spending equal amounts of time with each parent. You could agree to take turns claiming head of household. You would need to use the same care as with exemptions so you do not both claim both in a given year. You should also know that if you do file jointly, you won't be able to claim alimony (see "Alimony" below). Couples who file jointly cannot show alimony as a deduction to the paying spouse, or as income to the receiving spouse. Obviously, your filing status will need to be considered thoroughly if large alimony payments are to be made.

Refunds and Liabilities

If you decide to file jointly, you will need to discuss and decide on issues regarding refunds and liabilities. The basic questions are: If there is a refund, how will it be split? If there is a liability, how will that expense be split? Some couples choose to split by an agreed proportion: e.g., 50/50, 60/40, 70/30, etc. Others divide it up in proportion to income. You can mix and match these areas, splitting tax refunds one way, and tax liabilities another. (You may be thinking that you'll suggest a 50/50 split — you get the refunds and your spouse gets the liabilities — but that probably won't be looked on very kindly!)

Alimony

For individual taxpayers, alimony is a taxable event. That is, there are tax consequences for calling a support payment "alimony." Alimony is generally considered taxable income to the person receiving it and is deductible for the person paying it (there are some exceptions). This can be useful where there is a large disparity in incomes, since it means the person paying alimony saves tax dollars at a higher rate than the person receiving alimony pays tax dollars. This may make it possible for both of you to share in the savings, assuming you're working toward the best interests of both.

However, alimony is not a taxable event (as described above) if you file jointly. The IRS considers the payment and receipt of alimony a "wash" if you are co-mingling your funds and exemptions.

Betty Jean made far more money than her husband, **Doug**. Because of this, she suggested that, at income tax time, she be allowed to take the dependent exemptions on their three daughters. Doug responded that he needed as much tax break as Betty Jean and suggested they split the tax exemptions. Since there were three exemptions, they had a difficult time figuring out how to handle the situation until they hit upon the idea that they could each claim one exemption and alternate the other. That seemed workable until Betty Jean figured out that because of her vastly higher income she needed the exemptions in the short run to get the best break.

The couple finally agreed on the following formula: Betty Jean took two exemptions — for the two oldest children — and Doug took one — the youngest. While this gave Betty Jean the greater deduction immediately, her exemptions would run out sooner; Doug's exemption on the youngest child, while not equivalent to two at this point, would balance out because he would have the ability to claim the exemption longer.

Without much additional discussion, they were able to agree to file a joint return for the previous year. They recognized that filing jointly would offset any savings that might be accrued by the minimal alimony that Betty Jean had paid Doug in the previous year. They also agreed that for the following year they would check with their tax expert to determine whether filing individually or jointly would save both of them the most money. The spouse who saved most by filing singly would transfer some as a gift to the other, as a way of balancing out the savings. Finally, any refunds or liabilities for the past tax year would be split equally, and for the next tax year would be split proportionally to income. When they eventually divorced and could only file separately, taxes would be their individual responsibility.

If alimony is being paid, you will need to check to see if more than $15,000 per year is being transferred. If it is, it needs to continue for more than three years, according to the IRS (for settlements entered into after December 31, 1986). The IRS has certain regulations regarding how much can be claimed in what blocks of time. In this case, if the amount decreases by more than $15,000 between the 1st and second or 2nd and third year, the IRS may look at $15,000 per year at some type of tax-deductible property settlement "tax scam" if it does not continue for three years. Exceptions would include certain contingencies, such as death of either spouse, remarriage of the spouse receiving support or changes in income specified in the agreement. As you can see, these are potentially tricky and complex issues. It is a good idea to check with a CPA or accountant who has specific knowledge of divorce taxation if there is the least bit of doubt in your mind.

For married couples filing "separately," alimony will only be deductible (to the paying spouse) if certain language is used in the separation agreement and other requirements are met. Generally, alimony is a contingent event. That means it has to stop at some point, such as death of either party, or remarriage of person receiving alimony (there are some exceptions to this).

There are other contingencies that are also acceptable such as increase in income to dispose receiving support for a specified length of time for payment.

Check with your accountant or tax consultant if you need more information about any aspect of taxes. The laws and procedures are complex! And keep in mind also that Congress (and the fifty state legislatures) change the tax laws frequently. Be sure you're up to date!

(For example, as this is written in summer 2000, the U.S. House of Representatives has passed major changes in the so-called "marriage penalty" tax rules. If Congress sends such a bill on to the President, he has threatened a veto; an override appears doubtful. While this maneuvering may be dismissed as election year politics, the outcome may have major consequences for married couples filing jointly.)

Remember to write down, in as much detail as possible, the decisions you have made together, and keep copies handy for both of you to review for later consideration.

Information in this chapter has been verified by the accounting firm of Toal, Raines, Davis and Simmons, Certified Public Accountants of Annapolis, Maryland, as of June 2000. *Changes in federal tax law subsequent to publication, may render this material out of date. Please discuss your decisions about taxes and financial planning with a qualified tax expert!*

If you or your spouse have trouble with any of the issues in this chapter, contact a mediator or expert tax advisor for help.

10

Putting It All Together

(Don't Sign Anything Yet!)

I CONGRATULATE YOU ON YOUR PERSISTENCE (and good judgment) in working your way through the book to this point. You and your spouse have covered all of the *main* topics, but you have a few more simple things to do to complete your task. The first is to discuss any other areas that you feel would be useful to include in a separation agreement. We have already touched on the issues that are typical and useful to most families. Each family is unique, however, and usually has other issues that need to be covered. There may be issues specific to your situation that you will want to discuss. Now is the time to do it... *carefully*.

Other Topics
Keep in mind that it is more useful and more positive to discuss things that you both *agree to do*, rather than things that you *agree not to do*. (Statements about not having your current romantic interest over for dinner or overnight when the children are staying with you are typically meant as punitive controls, rather than as constructive arrangements). Most couples can operate on the assumption that neither spouse would knowingly or purposely put the children at risk or in jeopardy. That being the case, contractual arrangements of a negative nature are rarely useful or practical. Examples of positive topics that you might want to discuss include such major family events as the children's graduation from high school, college, marriage, grandchildren...

Is That All There Is?
It is not possible to cover all future contingencies. You can make yourself crazy trying to consider all of the "what ifs," and trying to write plans and agreements that cover them. It is far better to set

up periodic meetings to review and possibly renegotiate certain aspects of the contract. At that time, you can develop the schedule or the contingencies that would call for renegotiation. Significant changes in income, children reaching certain ages or educational milestones, and other major events are events that might trigger a renegotiation of the co-parenting or support agreements. Every one, two, or three years would be an appropriate schedule for renegotiation, even without major life changes.

What Happens When a Spouse Marries Again?

Remarriage of either spouse is a contingency that has many special implications for the entire family. Most divorced people do remarry, so you are advised to plan for the possibility. The subject is complex; indeed, whole books have been written on how to handle "expanded family" situations.

A plan for dealing with remarriage should take into account how the new marital status will affect the children and the ex-spouse. The commitments you have made to each other in earlier discussions regarding property, co-parenting, finances, and other areas must be honored. A new spouse (and perhaps family) may mean reduced contact time with your children, or it could mean a changed outlook on custody. You'll need to consider how your soon-to-be-ex spouse will feel about changes in your circumstances. Similarly, a new spouse could mean a change in your financial situation, and your ability to meet obligations agreed to in the divorce settlement. For example, will you expect your new spouse to help support your family? Will your ex-spouse's new spouse be responsible for supporting your children? If the support agreement has been based on one spouse's "ability to pay," will the creation of a new marriage be an acceptable reason to change the "ability to pay"? As with all other areas, discussion before the event — now, or at a specified time in the future — will help clear the way. If you reach agreements on how you will handle the remarriage of either or both spouses, it would be a good idea to write them down as a part of your overall agreement.

If all parties understand in advance what is going to take place, and how the changes will be handled, either spouse can make the momentous decision to remarry with greater confidence and less disruption in the lives of all concerned.

The Final Exam

Once you've covered all of the areas and issues you need to cover, it's time for review. A master copy of all of your understandings should be written up, and copies made for both spouses. You should then sit down with your partner and review each of the issues, item by item, to make sure that they accurately and appropriately reflect what it was you were trying to say and do. If, while you are going through your understandings, either you or your spouse want to make an adjustment or modification, that's okay. Once you see the "whole picture," you may see that something doesn't fit, or you may want to suggest a modification so something can work even better.

When the review is complete, you need to turn the list of understandings into a formal document. *DON'T SIGN ANYTHING AT THIS TIME!*

Making It Legal

It is now time to see an attorney. Depending on your situation, you may want to approach one attorney who may agree to talk to both of you and draft a separation agreement along the lines of the understandings that you have developed. Some attorneys will talk to both spouses on an informal basis. However, many attorneys are not willing to do this and will insist that each of you be represented separately. This is not necessarily bad. You should each know what your legal rights are and know what the legal ramifications of these tentative arrangements will be. An attorney is the only one who can tell you that.

You may wish to call around and speak with several attorneys, not only to find out what their rates are, but also to see how you feel about having them work for you. Remember, whether you get one or two attorneys, they are employed by you; they should do what you want, within the limits of their capabilities. (Two other books in this Rebuilding Books series have lots of good suggestions on selecting and working with attorneys. Take a look at *The Child Custody Book* by Judge James W. Stewart, and *Parenting After Divorce* by psychologist Philip Stahl.)

Attorneys are trained to represent you and get the best possible deal they can for you. While this is great for you, it may not be good for the family. If you and your spouse have talked things out and decided how you would like things to be, then you have the right to have those things occur that way, as long as it is not against the law and no one is being hurt. If you feel what you and your spouse have decided is fair, equitable, and right for your family, then you need to find someone who will help you set up the contract the way you desire. That is not to say if your attorney points out a pitfall or weakness in the set of understandings you have developed, that you are not able to go back and talk with your spouse about making changes. Rather, I am trying to warn you that, even if an attorney says you can get more, or that you don't have to pay that much, if you feel that your tentative agreement with your spouse is fair and appropriate for the family, that should be the deciding factor.

In any event, after you have spoken with your attorney(s), a formal separation agreement can ultimately be drawn up. You both should give the document a final careful review to be certain it says what you believe you agreed to, that it does in fact reflect decisions the two of you have made and are willing to live and abide by. Only then, when you are satisfied, should the agreement be signed by you and your spouse.

Once that is accomplished, you can give this book to someone else who is in need of help, unless you want to keep it for the list of resources or as a reminder of your hard work and successful achievement.

Closing Comments
We've been working together for quite a long time; I'm sure the process has not been easy. In fact, it has probably been painful at times. I hope, however, that this book has been helpful to you, and helped to make this a rewarding process. If you have followed the procedures described here, you and your spouse should have been able to develop a set of understandings that will become a workable, useful, and realistic separation agreement. That document will do what you want it to do, especially if you've built into it enough flexibility to allow for changes and modifications of those situations in life which none of us can possibly predict.

I would welcome any comments that you would care to write to me with regard to how you feel this book may be improved. If there are any areas that were unclear or incomplete, or if you and your spouse have come up with an idea that you believe is creative, unique, or helpful, please let me know and I will try to incorporate that information in future revisions. Address your comments and suggestions to me in care of Impact Publishers, Inc., P.O. Box 6016, Atascadero, California 93423-6016.

I wish you well.

Appendices

Appendix A
Agendas for Discussion

Agenda 1: Co-Parenting

A. Discuss information that will be shared concerning the children's health and education.

B. Discuss how medical emergencies will be handled and who can sign for them.

C. Explore how and when parents will communicate with each other.

D. Explore how and when parents will communicate with the children when the children are with the other parent.

E. Daily schedule: develop several possible contact schedules.

F. Combine alternative schedules into one (or more) useful day-to-day contact schedules.

G. If more than one schedule: set up contingencies for switching from one to the next.

H. List special days.

I. Discuss how special days will be handled.

J. List extended vacations: with and without the children.

K. Discuss contact and coverage for extended vacations

Agenda 2: Co-Parenting II

A. List significant others (grandparents, aunts, uncles, cousins, etc.) with whom the children may have contact.

B. Discuss what will happen if one parent dies: where and with whom will the children live; will the surviving parent enable the children to have contact with the deceased parent's family?

C. Explore and discuss how transportation for the children will take place: who will be responsible for pickup and drop-off?

D. Develop alternatives for dealing with sick children: who will take time off from work? will the children still follow the daily schedule?

E. List extracurricular activities in which the children are currently involved: list other extracurricular activities in which they may be involved in the future; discuss how decisions will be made concerning selection of extracurricular activities and how transportation to and from these activities will be accomplished.

F. Discuss how gifts to the children will be handled: are their limits? will you compare notes prior to purchase?

G. Discuss the purchase of children's clothing: who will be responsible for the purchase? how will the cost be handled?

H. Discuss the children's allowance: how much, who will pay?

I. Explore options for dealing with forgotten "stuff" left at the other parent's home.

J. Define moving: what will happen when moving occurs?

K. Discuss contingencies under which changes in coparenting would take place: change in residence, changing job; changing marital status.

Agenda 3: Co-Parenting III

A. Consider how frequently you would like to review the parenting plan and possibly renegotiate; what is the time frame? what is the date by which the negotiation will take place?

B. Discuss whether discipline will follow the child from household to household.

C. Discuss whether you will establish house rules for the children to follow: will the rules be the same or different in each household?

D. Discuss how major decisions will be made involving:

    1. education

    2. religion

    3. health

    4. behavior

    5. social activity

E. If the joint decision-making is considered: explore how ties will be broken in you cannot agree on a particular issue.

F. Discuss custody

    1. joint

    2. sole

    3. split

G. List any other considerations or concerns that have not been discussed so far that concern the children.

Agenda 4: Property

A. List all assets held by everyone in family.

B. List all debts (liabilities) held by everyone in family.

C. Value all assets.

D. Value all debts.

E. Consider resource help.

    1) Appraisers

    2) Real estate

    3) Other business

    4) Attorneys, other

F. Set aside non-marital assets.

G. Set aside assets to be held jointly, to go to children, or to go to others.

H. Divide remaining assets

I. Divide liabilities or assign responsibility for payment.

J. List assets and liabilities each retains.

K. List assets and liabilities to be held jointly.

Agenda 5: Support

A. Fill out budget forms (separately).

B. Combine budgets using

    1) Summary sheet

    2) Newsprint

    3) Computer spreadsheet

C. Compare proposed expenses with net income, both net and gross.

D. Review Budget for revising.

    1) Reduction

    2) Increase

E. Consider resource help.

    1) Financial manager

    2) Credit Counselor

    3)   Accountant

F. Discuss need to transfer money from one spouse to other.

G. Discuss alternatives for increasing income

H. Look at non-marital assets/income with regard to need.

I. Set up transfer amount

    1)   Child(ren) support

    2)   Spousal support

    3)   Special expenses

J. Discuss

    1)   Length of time support continues

    2)   Contingencies for change up or down

        a)   Cost of living

        b)   Remarriage

        c)   Death

        d)   Children's milestones: eighteenth birthday, graduation from high school, leaving home, going to college, other

Agenda 6: Insurance

Life Insurance

A. List all life insurance policies.

B. Divide into term and whole life policies.

C. Value insurance policies.

    1)   Face value

    2)   Cash value

D. List policies by owner.

E. Discuss coverage needed in light of projected expenses (support, college, etc.).

    1)   Policy on whose life?

    2)   Coverage for how long?

    3)   What amount of coverage?

    4)   How are beneficiaries protected?

a) Cross ownership

b) Irrevocable beneficiary

F. Consider resource experts

   1) Insurance salespeople

   2) Insurance consultants

   3) Financial planners

Health Insurance

A. List all policies and coverage (HMO).

B. Who is covered?

C. Who will pay for health insurance?

D. How long will coverage continue?

E. How will uninsured medical/dental expenses be covered by the parents?

Agenda 7: College Education (or Equivalent)

A. Discuss who needs additional (college) education.

B. For each, discuss

   1) When education will begin

   2) How long will it last

   3) What is covered (tuition, room. board, books, recreation)

   4) What is the projected expense

   5) How will that expense be covered

C. Where will education take place or what criteria will be used to choose

   1) An institution?

   2) A major?

   3) Course work?

D. What indexes will be used to protect the parents?

Agenda 8: Taxes

A.   What parts of support will be called

    1)   Alimony?

        a)   More that $15,000/year for three years or more?

    2)   Child Support?

B.   Who will claim exemptions?

    1)   Wife

    2)   Husband

    3)   Both

    4)   Alternate

    5)   Is a letter/document needed?

C.   How will tax returns be filed?

    1)   Separate

    2)   Joint

    3)   How long (what years)?

D.   How will refunds/liabilities be handled?

E.   Consider resource help:

    1)   Domestic tax specialist

    2)   Accountant

    3)   Tax attorney

Appendix B
Selected Bibliography

Ahrons, C.R. The binuclear family: two households, one family. *Alternative Lifestyles*, 1979, 2 (4), 499-515.

American Bar Association. *Law & Marriage: Your Legal Guide*. Chicago: American Bar Association, 1985.

Clements, J. *25 Myths You've Got to Avoid if You Want to Manage Your Money Right*. New York: Simon & Schuster, 1998.

Coulson, R. *Fighting Fair*. New York: The Free Press, 1983.

Ellis, A. *How to Make Yourself Happy and Remarkably Less Disturbable*. Atascadero, CA: Impact Publishers, 1999.

Fisher, B. & Alberti, R.E. *Rebuilding: When Your Relationship Ends*, 3rd Edition. Atascadero, CA: Impact Publishers, 1999.

Gardner, R. *The Boys and Girls Book About Divorce*. New York: Bantam Books, 1970.

Galper, M. *Co-parenting: Sharing Your Child Equally*. Philadelphia: Running Press, 1978.

Janik, C. & Rejnis, R. *All America's Real Estate Book*. New York: Viking, 1985.

Porter, S. *Sylvia Porter's Money Book*. New York: Bantam Books, 1987.

Prudential Insurance Company of America, *The Prudential Financial Planning Guide* (Katherine Barret, Editor). New York: Collier Books (Macmillan), 1985.

Ricci, I. *Mom's House, Dad's House: Making Shared Custody Work*. New York: Macmillan, 1980.

Salk, L. *What Every Child Would Like Parents to Know About Divorce*. New York: Harper and Row, 1978.

Schimmel, D. & Fischer, L. *The Rights of Parents in the Education of Their Children*. Columbia, MD: National Committee for Citizens in Education 1977. (Suite 410, Wilde Lake Village Green, 21044).

Stahl, P. *Parenting After Divorce: A Guide to Resolving Conflicts and Meeting Your Children's Needs*. Atascadero, CA: Impact Publishers, 2000.

Stewart, J.W. *The Child Custody Book: How To Protect Your Children and Win Your Case*. Atascadero, CA: Impact Publishers, 2000.

Stewart. J.W. *Divorce Handbook for California: How to Dissolve Your Marriage Without Disaster*. Atascadero, CA: Impact Publishers, 1999.

Wallerstein, J. & Kelly, J.D. *Surviving the Breakup: How Children and Parents Cope With Divorce*. New York: Basic Books, 1980.

Walton, B.J. *101 Little Instructions for Surviving Your Divorce: A No-Nonsense Guide to the Challenges at Hand*. Atascadero, CA: Impact Publishers, 1999.

Ware, C. *Sharing Parenthood After Divorce*. New York: The Viking Press, 1982.

Watson, M.A. Custody alternatives: Defining the best interest of the children. *Family Relationships*. 1981, 30, 474-479.

Webb, D. *50 Ways to Love Your Leaver: Getting on With Your Life After the Breakup*. Atascadero, CA: Impact Publishers, 1999.

Weiss, R. *Marital Separation*. New York: Basic Books, 1975.

Wells, T. *Keeping Your Cool Under Fire: Communicating Non-defensively*. New York: McGraw-Hill, 1980.

Appendix C
Monthly Expense Budget Worksheet

	Yourself	Children
Regular Monthly Expenses:		
Housing:		
Rent	_____	_____
House Payments:		
Principal and Interest	_____	_____
Real Estate Taxes	_____	_____
Home Insurance	_____	_____
Other (specify) _____	_____	_____
Utilities:		
Electricity	_____	_____
Gas/Heating Oil	_____	_____
Telephone	_____	_____
Internet/Cable	_____	_____
Water	_____	_____
Installment Debt Payments	_____	_____
Household Operation & Maintenance:		
Repairs	_____	_____
Dry Cleaning & Laundry	_____	_____
Domestic Help:		
(____days at $ _____ per day)	_____	_____
Children's Day Care	_____	_____
Other (specify) _____	_____	_____
_____	_____	_____
Daily Expenses:		
Food:		
At home	_____	_____
Away from home *(amounts not reimbursed)*	_____	_____
Clothing *(including working clothes)*	_____	_____
Transportation:		
Gas and Oil *(amounts not reimbursed)*	_____	_____
Auto Repair & Maintenance	_____	_____
Other (bus, taxi, parking...)	_____	_____

Health, Medical, and Dental:

Medical, Dental & Hospital Insurance
(Note but don't count payroll deduction) ⸻⸻   ⸻⸻

Medical & Health Care
(not covered by insurance) ⸻⸻   ⸻⸻

Dental ⸻⸻   ⸻⸻

Medicines & Drugs ⸻⸻   ⸻⸻

Other (Therapy, etc.) ⸻⸻   ⸻⸻

Education, Self & Children:
(Current)

Private School Tuition ⸻⸻   ⸻⸻

College Tuition ⸻⸻   ⸻⸻

Books and Fees ⸻⸻   ⸻⸻

Other (specify) ⸻⸻⸻⸻ ⸻⸻   ⸻⸻

Variable Monthly Expenses:

Drug/Variety ⸻⸻   ⸻⸻

Magazines, Books, Newspapers ⸻⸻   ⸻⸻

Children's Allowances ⸻⸻   ⸻⸻

Charities, Gifts, Contributions ⸻⸻   ⸻⸻

Dues *(not included as business expenses)* ⸻⸻   ⸻⸻

Cultural/Recreational ⸻⸻   ⸻⸻

Veterinary Expenses ⸻⸻   ⸻⸻

Hair Care and Clothing ⸻⸻   ⸻⸻

Seasonal (see below)

TOTAL MONTHLY EXPENSES ⸻⸻   ⸻⸻

Seasonal Expenses:

Automobile Insurance ⸻⸻   ⸻⸻

Life Insurance ⸻⸻   ⸻⸻

Disability insurance ⸻⸻   ⸻⸻

Taxes (Auto Tags) ⸻⸻   ⸻⸻

ANNUAL TOTAL ⸻⸻   ⸻⸻

MONTHLY AVERAGE TOTAL
(Divide Annual by 12) ⸻⸻   ⸻⸻

Budget Summary

	W	C	H	C
Rent/Mortgage				
Electricity				
Gas/Oil				
Telephone				
Internet/Cable				
Water				
Installment Payment				
Food At Home				
Food — Away				
Clothing				
Gasoline				
Auto Repair				
Bus/Metro				
Med/Dent Insurance				
Medical Not Insured				
Dental Not Insured				
Medication/Drugs				
Household Repairs				
Laundry/Cleaning				
Child Day Care				
Education - Tuition				
Education – Books				
Education – Other				
Variety				
Books, Paper				
Allowance				
Gifts/Contributions				
Dues				
Recreation				
Veterinary Care				
Hair Care				
Seasonal Expenses				
TOTAL				

Grand Totals

Expenses   Income

    Wife/child   _____   Wife   _____

    Husband/child   _____   Husband   _____

    Total Expense   _____   Total Income   _____

        RESULT (Total Income less Total Expenses) _____

Appendix D
Financial Information and Income Statement

(The following list is only meant to help you get started. It is not meant to be all-inclusive. You may have other assets and liabilities; be sure to list them as well.)

Assets	Value	In Whose Name

Real Estate
Residence _____ _____
Vacation property _____ _____
Business property _____ _____
Other_____ _____ _____

Bank Accounts *(Specify)*
Savings

_____ _____ _____
_____ _____ _____

Checking

_____ _____ _____
_____ _____ _____

Accounts Receivable *(Specify)*
(Money owed to you)

_____ _____ _____
_____ _____ _____

Stock/Bonds/Mutual Funds *(Specify)*

_____ _____ _____

Pension/IRA/Keough/SEP *(Specify)*

_____ _____ _____
_____ _____ _____

Business/Professional Practice (Specify)

_____ _____ _____
_____ _____ _____

Life Insurance (Specify company, policy #)

_____ _____ _____
_____ _____ _____

Valuable Personal Property (Enter value; attach lists)

Cars/Trucks _____ _____
Boats _____ _____
Campers _____ _____
Collections _____ _____
Art _____ _____
Investment Jewelry _____ _____
Hobby equipment _____ _____
Tools _____ _____
Musical instruments _____ _____
Cemetery plots _____ _____
Season passes/tickets _____ _____
Computers/Electronics _____ _____
Oriental rugs _____ _____
Other _____ _____

Liabilities   Amount   In Whose Name
Mortgages (Specify)

_____   _____   _____
_____   _____   _____

Loans (Specify)
Bank

_____   _____   _____

_____   _____   _____
Personal

_____   _____   _____

_____   _____   _____

Insurance Policy

_____   _____   _____

_____   _____   _____

Income Tax
Year _____   _____   _____
Year _____   _____   _____

Credit Cards (Specify Companies)

_____   _____   _____
_____   _____   _____
_____   _____   _____

Liens

_____   _____   _____

Income   H   W
   Gross Yearly Income   _____   _____
   Gross Monthly Income   _____   _____

Subtract payroll deductions
   Health insurance   _____   _____
   Pension   _____   _____
   Life insurance   _____   _____
   FICA   _____   _____
   State tax   _____   _____
   Federal tax   _____   _____
   Other

Other Monthly Income
   Self employment   _____   _____
   Dividends   _____   _____
   Interest   _____   _____
   Trusts   _____   _____
   Rents   _____   _____
   Royalties   _____   _____
   Other_____   _____   _____

Deductions
   Estimated /mo.   _____   _____

TOTAL NET MONTHLY
   (spendable cash)   _____   _____

Appendix E

Resources for Finding a Professional Mediator

Check your local "yellow pages" under;

>Mediation
>
>Marriage & Family Therapy
>
>Lawyers/Attorneys

or contact one of the following professional organizations:

Academy of Family Mediators
P.O. Box 4686
Greenwich, CT 06830
(203) 629-8049

Association of Family & Conciliation Courts (AFCC)
2680 Southwest Glen Eagles Road
Lake Oswego, Oregon 97304

divorcesource.com

mirc.com

Society of Professionals in Dispute Resolution (SPIDR)
1730 Rhode Island Ave., N.W.
Suite 509
Washington, DC 20036
(202) 833-2188

Appendix F
Children's Data Sheet

Name_____ Date of Birth_____

Grade_____ School_____ Phone_____

Teacher_____ Principal_____

School Schedule: Opens_____ Closes_____

After School Activities:_____

Schedule for Activities:_____

Doctor_____ Phone_____

Allergies_____ Health Concerns_____

Medications_____ Blood Type_____

Health Insurance Provider_____ Phone_____

Health Insurance ID #_____ SSN#_____

Bed Time:_____ Bath Schedule:_____

Favorite Foods:_____

Clothes Sizes: Shirts _____ Pants _____ Shoes _____ Socks _____

Underwear _____ Pants _____ Dress _____ Coat _____

Other:_____

Friends:

Name_____ Phone _____

Parents _____

Name_____ Phone _____

Parents _____

Name_____ Phone _____

Parents _____

Name_____ Phone _____

Parents _____

Index

child, 107-112
cost of living adjustments (COLA),
   105-107
income and, 102-103
negotiating levels of, 103-104
spousal, 112-116
Sylvia Porter's Money Book, 149

— T —

Tax exemptions, 149-151
Tie-breaker, 61-62
Toal, Raines, Davis, and Simmons,
   CPAs, 155
Transportation, 37-39

— V —

Visa, 84

— W —

Wal-Mart, 24
Ware, C., 12

— Y —

"You" statements, 5

CPSIA information can be obtained at www.ICGtesting.com
Printed in the USA
LVOW07s0051240815

451272LV00003B/22/P

9 781886 230217